MW01042023

Windows XP
Unwired

Other Windows resources from O'Reilly

Related titles

Mac OS X Unwired

Wireless Hacks

Building Wireless
  Community Networks

Windows XP in a
  Nutshell

Windows XP
  Annoyances

Windows XP Pocket
  Reference

Windows XP Hacks

Linux Unwired

**Windows Books
Resource Center**

windows.oreilly.com is a complete catalog of O'Reilly's Windows and Office books, including sample chapters and code examples.

oreillynet.com is the essential portal for developers interested in open and emerging technologies, including new platforms, programming languages, and operating systems.

Conferences

O'Reilly & Associates brings diverse innovators together to nurture the ideas that spark revolutionary industries. We specialize in documenting the latest tools and systems, translating the innovator's knowledge into useful skills for those in the trenches. Visit *conferences.oreilly.com* for our upcoming events.

Safari Bookshelf (*safari.oreilly.com*) is the premier online reference library for programmers and IT professionals. Conduct searches across more than 1,000 books. Subscribers can zero in on answers to time-critical questions in a matter of seconds. Read the books on your Bookshelf from cover to cover or simply flip to the page you need. Try it today with a free trial.

Windows XP
Unwired

A Guide for Home, Office, and the Road

Wei-Meng Lee

O'REILLY®

Beijing · Cambridge · Farnham · Köln · Paris · Sebastopol · Taipei · Tokyo

Windows XP Unwired
by Wei-Meng Lee

Published by O'Reilly & Associates, Inc., 1005 Gravenstein Highway North,
Sebastopol, CA 95472.

O'Reilly & Associates books may be purchased for educational, business, or sales pro-
motional use. Online editions are also available for most titles (*safari.oreilly.com*). For
more information, contact our corporate/institutional sales department: (800) 998-9938
or *corporate@oreilly.com*.

Editor:	Brian Jepson
Production Editor:	Mary Brady
Cover Designer:	Edie Freedman
Interior Designer:	David Futato

Printing History:

August 2003:	First Edition.

ISBN: 0-596-00536-9

[C]

Table of Contents

Preface

With the explosive growth of the Internet, more and more people got connected. The world suddenly became much smaller, because the distance between people from different parts of the world no longer prevented them from collaborating. In the 90s, there was a frenzied race to get people and corporations connected. Today, Internet access is a necessity; even novice users have trouble finding value in a computer that doesn't have email, a web browser, or instant messenger (IM).

While Internet access becomes as important as telephone or cable service, even more demanding users are appearing who are not satisfied in just getting connected. They want flexible ways to get connected wherever they take their notebook computers.

When wireless networking became affordable, early adopters installed it in their homes and offices, and it also quickly became a part of life in other places: many Starbucks Coffee and Borders bookstores now include wireless hotspots, mobile users are reading and sending email over cellular networks, and students are learning with notebook computers equipped with wireless network cards.

Today, wireless devices come in all shapes and sizes. In fact, wireless technology is not something new: remote control cars and TV remote controls have been in use for some time. Wireless technologies have penetrated our lives for so long that we take them for granted. In the case of a TV remote controller, infrared technology (which uses light) carries signals across the room. For the remote control car, radio waves transmit information from the controller to the car.

What This Book Covers

This book explains the following wireless technologies and how to use them with a Windows XP computer:

Wireless Fidelity (Wi-Fi)

Wi-Fi is sometimes called "wireless Ethernet." Using Wi-Fi, you can connect to the Internet without wires and roam from place to place (within range of the network) while maintaining your connection. Wi-Fi uses radio waves to transmit information. Chapters 1, 2, 3, 4, and 5 discuss Wi-Fi.

Bluetooth

Bluetooth is often touted as a cable-replacement technology. Like Wi-Fi, Bluetooth also uses radio waves but operates within a shorter range. It is ideal for replacing cables that connect two devices. For example, your keyboard and mouse can use Bluetooth technology to transmit signals to your computer, eliminating unsightly cables that often get hopelessly tangled. You can also wirelessly synchronize your PDA with your computer via Bluetooth. Chapter 6 discusses Bluetooth.

Infrared

Infrared technology has been with us for a number of years. Infrared requires line of sight (LOS) to transmit data. Infrared is a short-range wireless technology like Bluetooth, but it uses light waves that are just outside the spectrum of visible light rather than radio waves. Chapter 7 discusses Infrared.

General Packet Radio Services (GPRS) and Code Division Multiple Access 2000 (CDMA2000)

While Wi-Fi allows you to connect to the network wirelessly, it has limited coverage. Physically moving out of range of a wireless network breaks the connection. In highly mobile situations, GPRS and CDMA2000 may be the ideal solution (or a complement to Wi-Fi for network connectivity when you're away from a hotspot). CDMA2000 and GPRS are two leading networking technologies used by high-speed (at the time of this writing, 50 to 70 Kbps; sometimes higher) cellular networking called 3G (which stands for third-generation, but it is usually called 2.5G because the current technology didn't quite live up to the high speeds originally promised). As long as you are within reach of a cell tower, either protocol will keep you connected to the network (and Internet).

The choice of CDMA2000 or GPRS is generally dictated by your choice of wireless provider. For example, AT&T Wireless and T-Mobile both use GPRS for their 2.5G cellular networking, while Sprint and Verizon

Wireless use CDMA2000. At the time of this writing, unlimited CDMA2000 data plans are available for $80 a month in the United States, but only T-Mobile offers flat-rate GPRS pricing ($80 gets you around 60 MB with AT&T; T-Mobile offers unlimited GPRS for as little as $20 a month). Chapter 8 discusses cellular networking. (Chapter 6 shows how you can connect to the Internet using a Bluetooth-enabled cell phone as a modem, and Chapter 7 does the same, but with Infrared).

Besides talking about the various wireless technologies, this book also covers some of their uses:

Emergence of wireless hotspots
A wireless hotspot is a specific location where you can connect to the Internet wirelessly using Wi-Fi. Some wireless hotspots include your favorite Starbucks Coffee, Burger King, McDonald's, and Delifrance outlets. With wireless hotspots, you can now work, sip some coffee, and engage in people-watching all at the same time. Chapter 3 discusses connecting to wireless hotspots.

Global Positioning System (GPS)
GPS is a technology that has many commercial and academic uses. Using a GPS receiver and relevant mapping software, delivery personnel can quickly locate a destination with the aid of the navigational software. A GPS device works by reading the data emitted by satellites orbiting around the earth and calculating the destination's precise location on earth. Chapter 9 discusses GPS.

Microsoft Smart Display
One of the dream uses of wireless technology is the ability to work anywhere in the comfort of your home. Until Microsoft started shipping its Smart Display product, this was only available to laptop users. With a Smart Display, you can detach your monitor from your desktop computer and work or play wirelessly in the comfort of your own home. Chapter 10 discusses Microsoft Smart Display.

Wireless Security

With the convenience of wireless technologies comes a new host of security problems. Unlike wired networks where security involves limiting physical access to routers, hubs, and cables, wireless networks' most vulnerable point (the radio waves floating through the air) has no physical substance, so securing wireless networks is a challenging task.

In this book, I take a look at the various ways to secure wireless networks, using standards such as Wired Equivalent Privacy (WEP), Wireless Protected Access (WPA), 802.1X, and 802.11i.

In addition, I also look at the security features found in the Bluetooth and Infrared technologies. Chapter 4 discusses what you need to know to communicate securely.

Conventions Used in This Book

This book uses the following abbreviations:

Hz, kHz, MHz, and GHz
> Hertz (cycles per second), KiloHertz (one thousand Hertz), MegaHertz (one million Hertz), and GigaHertz (one billion, or 10^9 Hertz).

bps, Kbps, Mbps
> Bits per second, kilobits (1024 bits) per second, and megabits (1,048,576 bits) per second.

KB/s, MB/s
> Kilobytes (1024 bytes) per second and megabytes (1,048,576 bytes) per second.

This book uses the following typographic conventions:

Constant width
> Constant width is used for listing the output of command-line utilities and for command names.

Constant width italic
> Constant width italic is used to show items that need to be replaced in commands.

Italic
> Italic is used for emphasis, for first use of a technical term, and for URLs.

...
> Ellipses indicate text that has been omitted for clarity.

 This icon indicates a tip, suggestion, or general note.

 This icon indicates a warning or caution.

Comments and Questions

Please address any comments or questions concerning this book to the publisher:

O'Reilly & Associates
1005 Gravenstein Highway North
Sebastopol, CA 95472
800-998-9938 (in the U.S. or Canada)
707-829-0515 (international or local)
707-829-0104 (fax)

To ask technical questions or comment on the book, send email to:

bookquestions@oreilly.com

We have a web site for this book where examples, errata, and any plans for future editions are listed. You can access this site at:

http://www.oreilly.com/catalog/winxpunwired

For more information about this book and others, see the O'Reilly web site:

http://www.oreilly.com

Readers who would like to contact the author to ask questions are welcome to do so at *wei_meng_lee@hotmail.com.* You may also read the author's O'Reilly Network Articles at *http://www.oreillynet.com/pub/au/944.*

Acknowledgments

The first section I turn to whenever I pick up a technical book is the Acknowledgments. This section tells you who the real heroes behind the scenes are. Though only my name appears on the cover, it is actually the collective efforts of many people that have made this book possible.

First and foremost, I want to express a heartfelt thank you to my editor, Brian Jepson. Brian has been instrumental in designing the Unwired series and making sure that the book you are holding in your hands is useful to you in your journey through the wireless world. Without Brian's help, this book would never have been possible. He has served both as an editor as well as an expert technical reviewer, raising questions that made me think deeper. Brian also contributed several sections to this book, covering areas that were just too much for me. For these, I am forever indebted to you, Brian. Thanks!

I am also grateful to John Osborn, who had the faith to sign me up with O'Reilly. Thanks, John! Thanks also to the many wonderful folks that I met at the O'Reilly Cambridge office when I was in the States in 2002.

This book covers a lot of products from many vendors. There is no way that I could own all these products, and was lent several for review purposes. For this, I would like to express my gratitude to the following people and companies for their generosity:

- Mr. Goh Joon Tai from EastRep Pte Ltd, for loaning me the Bluetake Bluetooth equipment.
- Mr. George Wong from D-Link International Pte Ltd, for loaning me the D-Link wireless access points, cards, and adapters.
- Ms. Jaylyn Tey and Ms. Janice Chew from ViewSonic Singapore Pte Ltd, for loaning me the ViewSonic AirPanel V150.
- Vera Lam and John Cheong of Space Machine, Inc., for loaning me the Pocket Map GPS.
- J. Abra Degbor of Verizon Wireless, for loaning me the Sierra Wireless Aircard 555 1xRTT wireless card.
- Suzanne Lammers and Amy Schiska of Sprint, for loaning me a PCS Vision card for their 1xRTT network.
- Ms. Jasmine Yong from Sony Ericsson Mobile Communications International AB, for loaning the T610 and the HBH-60 headset.

Thanks also to the various vendors who have kindly given me the permission to use the images of their products in this book.

Last, but not least, I would like to thank my family for their continuous support and understanding as I worked late into the nights.

CHAPTER ONE

Wireless Networking Fundamentals

To understand Wireless Networking, there are two things that are fundamental: Transmission Control Protocol/Internet Protocol (TCP/IP) and
radio waves. TCP/IP governs how data flows across the Internet, whether it
is over a dial-up modem, a cable modem, or a wireless network. Radio
waves surround us; some carry useful information, others are just noise.
This book is more concerned with the former, but the noise is of interest
too, since it can drown out the useful signals. The first half of this chapter
explains TCP/IP, and the second discusses radio waves. The rest of this
book looks at how the two work together.

TCP/IP

Most of the concepts presented in this book require a basic understanding of
TCP/IP, the networking standard used by the Internet as well as home or
office connections. To understand TCP/IP, you'll need to know how computers identify one another (IP addresses), talk to their immediate neighbors (subnet addressing), and talk to machines on the Internet or other
networks (routing).

IP Address

TCP/IP stands for Transmission Control Protocol/Internet Protocol. It is a
set of *protocols* that enable computers on the network to communicate with
one another. (A protocol defines how data is transmitted between computers; if both computers adhere to the same protocol, they can exchange data.)

On a TCP/IP network, each computer (also called a *host*) has an IP address.
An IP address is much like a Social Security number: it uniquely identifies
each computer on the network. An IP address has four numbers separated by
periods and looks like this: 192.168.1.2. Each number occupies 8 bits (1 byte)

and thus can range from 0 to 255 (although there are some combinations that are reserved and have special meanings). Each IP address takes up 4 bytes.

By convention, an IP address contains two components, as shown in Figure 1-1.

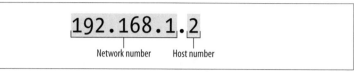

Figure 1-1. Components of an IP address

The first is the *network number*, and the second is the *host number*. Hosts that are on the same physical network normally share the same network number. There are five classes of IP address, indicated by the value of the *first byte* of the IP address:

Class A
> 0 to 127: Each Class A network supports a maximum of 16,777,214 hosts. Though there are a total of 128 network numbers here, only 125 are usable.

Class B
> 128 to 191: Each Class B network supports a maximum of 65,534 hosts. A total of 16,382 Class B networks are available.

Class C
> 192 to 223: Each Class C network supports 254 hosts. A total of 2,097,150 Class C hosts are available.

Class D
> 224 to 239: These networks are reserved for multicast addressing, which supports broadcasting the same data to multiple hosts.

Class E
> 240 to 254: These networks are reserved for experimental use.

The following IP address ranges are reserved for special purposes and hence are not used to assign to any host (for a complete list of special-use addresses, see *http://www.ietf.org/rfc/rfc3330.txt?number=3330*):

0.0.0.0 to 0.255.255.255
> Broadcast addresses. These are used to send traffic to hosts on the current network.

127.0.0.0 to 127.255.255.255
> Loopback addresses. 127.0.0.1 is used to loop back to the current host (so if you try to make a network connection to that address, you are talking to yourself).

169.254.0.0 to 169.254.255.255

Link local addresses. These are used for hosts that have to assign their own IP addresses.

The protocols used on the Internet are defined in a collection of notes called RFCs (Requests for Comments). For more information, see *http://www.rfc-editor.org/*.

The following IP addresses are reserved for private networks (such as a home network). These private networks can be configured to see the outside world (see "IP Routing" later in this chapter, as well as the sidebar "DHCP and NAT" in Chapter 5) without letting the outside world see them:

- 10.0.0.0 to 10.255.255.255
- 169.254.0.0 to 169.254.255.255
- 172.16.0.0 to 172.31.255.255
- 192.168.0.0 to 192.168.255.255

Figure 1-2 shows the Network number and Host number used in each class of IP addresses.

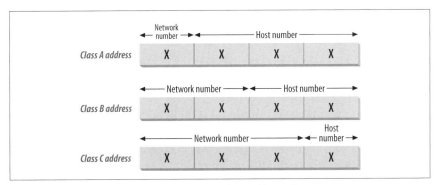

Figure 1-2. Network and Host numbers in each IP address class

IP Subnet Addressing

If you have ever manually configured a computer for TCP/IP networking, two of the configuration values are the IP address and a number called a *subnet mask*. If your network uses automatic configuration (see the sidebar "DHCP and NAT" in Chapter 5), then the IP address and subnet mask are automatically assigned to your computer.

To calculate a network number from an IP address, you can apply the subnet mask to it using Boolean arithmetic. For example, consider the IP address 192.168.1.2. This is a class C network and thus the first three numbers represent the network number. To derive the network number, we apply a subnet mask of 255.255.255.0 (or 11111111.11111111.11111111. 00000000 in binary). Performing an AND operation between the IP address and the subnet mask gives:

```
        11000000 10101000 00000001 00000010
AND     11111111.11111111.11111111.00000000
  =     11000000 10101000 00000001 00000000
  =       192.    168.     1.        0
```

The result (192.168.1.0) is the network number. Table 1-1 shows the default subnet mask for the three classes of networks.

Table 1-1. The default subnet masks for the three classes of networks

Address class	Subnet mask in bits	Subnet mask value
Class A	11111111 00000000 00000000 00000000	255.0.0.0
Class B	11111111 11111111 00000000 00000000	255.255.0.0
Class C	11111111 11111111 11111111 00000000	255.255.255.0

Subnets are sometimes specified using the network number and number of bits in the subnet mask. So, the Class C example in Table 1-1 with a network number of 192.168.1.0 would be written 192.168.1.0/24 because there are 24 bits in the subnet mask.

Supernet Addressing

Subnetting can be a wasteful way to allocate IP addresses. Consider a company that has more than 254 hosts: in theory, they would need a Class B IP address. But a Class B address can support 65,534 hosts; any remaining IP addresses would go unused, wasting a limited resource.

Instead of using a Class B address, you can instead combine a few Class C addresses into a *supernet*. Suppose you have about 700 hosts. You would need to obtain three Class C addresses such as:

- 192.168.1.0
- 192.168.2.0
- 192.168.3.0

Each Class C address can support up to 254 hosts, so three Class C addresses are sufficient to support 700 hosts. But how do all the hosts know that they are in the same supernet? The answer lies in the subnet mask again. Let's examine the binary equivalent of the IP addresses just listed:

```
192.168.1.0    11000000 10101000 00000001 00000000
192.168.2.0    11000000 10101000 00000010 00000000
192.168.3.0    11000000 10101000 00000011 00000000
```

The binary patterns are all similar up to the first 22 bits.

So our subnet mask now becomes 11111111 11111111 11111100 00000000, or 255.255.252.0.

IP Routing

Let's now discuss how data packets (short blocks of data used to transfer information) are transmitted between networks. Consider the first case where there are two computers on the same physical network (see Figure 1-3).

Figure 1-3. Two computers in a physical network

When A wants to send a packet to B, it first must know B's IP address (see Figure 1-4). But to actually move data to B, A also needs to know the Ethernet address (also known as the MAC—Media Access Control—address) of B. (An Ethernet address looks like this: 05-EF-45-4D-2E-A5.)

To find out the Ethernet address of another computer, the Address Resolution Protocol (ARP) is used. ARP keeps a table containing a list of IP addresses and their corresponding Ethernet addresses (you can list the contents of this table by running the command arp -a at the Windows XP

Command Prompt). If the table contains the Ethernet address of B, then A simply sends the packet over to B. If the table does not have an entry, A broadcasts an ARP query ("Who has the IP address 192.168.1.2?") to all the computers in the network. B will respond with its Ethernet address, which is then stored in A's ARP table. A can now send the packet over to B.

What happens if A needs to send packets to another computer on another physical network? ARP can't cross network boundaries, so a router takes care of moving data between networks (see Figure 1-4).

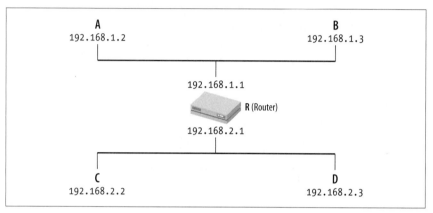

Figure 1-4. Using a router in two physical networks

If A is sending packets to B, it does so using the method just described. If A needs to send packets to D, it uses the following steps:

1. A uses ARP to find R's Ethernet address.
2. A sends the packets to R, but specifies D as the final destination.
3. R uses ARP to find D's Ethernet address.
4. R passes the packet to D.

Note that a router has more than one IP address, since it is connected to multiple physical networks. So, A and B know R as 192.168.1.1, and C and D know it as 192.168.2.1.

If you want to watch ARP resolution in action, launch the Ethereal protocol analyzer (see Chapter 4) and do the following:

1. Select Capture → Start.
2. Select the network adaptor that is connected to the network you want to monitor.
3. Set the filter to arp and click OK.

4. Open the Windows XP Command Prompt, and run the command `arp -d` *ip-address* (where *ip-address* is the IP address of the computer you want to connect to) to remove if from your computer's ARP cache; this forces it to broadcast the ARP request the next time you try to connect.

5. Ping the computer using `ping` *ip-address* at the Windows XP Command Prompt.

When the ping is complete, return to Ethereal, click Stop in the Capture window, and examine the log of ARP requests in Ethereal's main window. You should see the request and response, assuming that a computer with the *ip-address* exists on your local network and is currently up.

Domain Name System (DNS)

Identifying computers on the network (and on the Internet) by IP address is not particularly human-friendly. Just as you are addressed by your name (rather than your Social Security number), computers on the Internet are commonly addressed using *domain names*. Some examples of domain names are *www.amazon.com*, *www.google.com*, and *www.oreilly.com*.

Instead of using IP addresses, we use domain names that are meaningful and easy to remember. A DNS server is a database that contains the list of IP addresses and their corresponding domain names. Because the database is huge, it is not practical for a single machine to host all the domain names. Hence DNS is inherently *distributed*—there are many DNS servers on the Internet, and each of them can turn some of the world's domain names into IP addresses.

When you type *www.oreilly.com* into your browser, your computer first obtains the IP address of *www.oreilly.com* by querying a DNS server (usually your ISP's or organization's DNS server). If that DNS server does not contain an entry for the domain name, it then looks it up on other DNS servers that may contain an entry for *www.oreilly.com*. Ultimately one of these servers will find the IP address; if not, you'll get an error message.

> To find out the DNS server(s) that you use for your network, use the command `ipconfig /all` at the Windows XP Command Prompt. You can use the `nslookup` utility (which also displays your DNS server) to send queries to your DNS server interactively.

Limitations of IP Addressing

The current version of IP addressing is Version 4, or IPv4. IPv4 uses 32 bits for addressing. If all the possible addresses are allocated, there would be at most 2^{32} hosts, which is about 4.3 billion (4,294,967,296) addresses (not forgetting that a portion of these addresses are reserved for special purposes). Even with 4.3 billion addresses, it was estimated that we would still run out of IP addresses by the year 2008 (or the year 2028, depending on whose estimates you are looking at).

Though many schemes have been devised to prolong the "life" of IPv4, such as supernetting and Network Address Translation (NAT; see the sidebar "DHCP and NAT" in Chapter 5), the industry is looking towards using IPv6, which supports 128-bit addressing (2^{128} different addresses).

Multihomed Hosts

A host that has two IP addresses is known as a multihomed host. A router that is attached to two physical networks is an example of this.

Understanding Radio Waves

Most of the wireless technologies mentioned in the last section make use of radio waves. Wi-Fi, GPRS, GPS, and Bluetooth all utilize radio waves to transmit signals.

Radio Wave Basics

Put simply, a radio wave is an electromagnetic wave. It can propagate through a vacuum, air, liquid, or even solid objects. It can be depicted mathematically as a sinusoidal curve as shown in Figure 1-5.

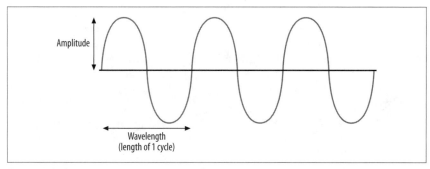

Figure 1-5. A sine wave representing a radio wave

The distance covered by a complete sine wave (a cycle) is known as the *wavelength*. The height of the wave is called the *amplitude*. The number of cycles made in a second is known as the *frequency*. Frequency is measured in Hertz (Hz), also known as cycles per second. So, a 1 Hz signal makes a full cycle once per second. You should be familiar with this unit of measurement: if your new computer operates at 2 GHz, the internal clock of your CPU generates signals at roughly two billion cycles per second.

 Note that frequency is inversely proportional to the wavelength—the longer the wavelength, the lower the frequency; the higher the frequency, the lower the wavelength. The wavelength of a 1 Hz signal is about 30 billion centimeters, which is the distance that light travels in one second. A 1 MHz signal has a wavelength of 300 meters.

Modulating Radio Waves

The sine wave carries data. To receive the transmission (such as audio or video), a radio wave receiver needs to tune itself to the same frequency as the transmitter. The receiver examines the amplitude or the frequency of the received electromagnetic wave in order to get at the transmitted data.

In the next section, I discuss three ways to carry data using radio waves.

Pulse Modulation. *Pulse Modulation* (PM) works by switching the radio signals ON and OFF (see Figure 1-6). This is similar to sending information using Morse code. The atomic clock set up by the National Institute of Standards and Technology in Fort Collins, Colorado uses PM to synchronize remote clocks and watches.

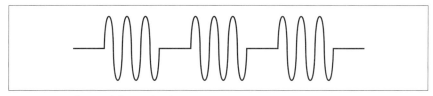

Figure 1-6. Pulse Modulation (PM)

Amplitude Modulation. *Amplitude Modulation* (AM), as the name implies, works by varying the amplitude of the sine waves (see Figure 1-7). Different amplitudes represent different values. The most famous example use of AM is in your radio.

Frequency Modulation. *Frequency Modulation* (FM) varies the frequency (the wavelength) of the sine waves (see Figure 1-8). The frequency of the sine waves changes slightly to represent different values. FM is commonly used in radios as well as popular household items such as televisions and cordless phones. Your mobile phone also uses FM.

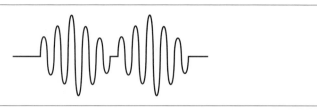

Figure 1-7. Amplitude Modulation (AM)

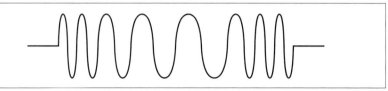

Figure 1-8. Frequency Modulation (FM)

Radio Frequency Spectrum

To regulate the use of the various radio frequencies, the Federal Communications Commission (FCC) in the United States determines the allocation of frequencies for various uses. Table 1-2 shows some of the bands defined by the FCC (see *http://www.fcc.gov/oet/spectrum/table/fcctable.pdf*).

Table 1-2. Range of frequencies defined for the various bands

Frequency	Band
10 kHz to 30 kHz	Very Low Frequency (VLF)
30 kHz to 300 kHz	Low Frequency (LF)
300 kHz to 3 MHz	Medium Frequency (MF)
3 MHz to 30 MHz	High Frequency (HF)
30 MHz to 328.6 MHz	Very High Frequency (VHF)
328.6 MHz to 2.9 GHz	Ultra High Frequency (UHF)
2.9 GHz to 30 GHz	Super High Frequency (SHF)
30 GHz and above	Extremely High Frequency (EHF)

Table 1-3 shows some example of radio devices and their frequency ranges.

Table 1-3. Some common radio devices and their frequency ranges

Frequency range	Device
535 kHz to 1.705 MHz	AM radio
5.95 MHz to 26.1 MHz	Short wave radio
54 to 88 MHz	Television stations (channels 2 through 6)
88 MHz to 108 MHz	FM radio

Table 1-3. Some common radio devices and their frequency ranges (continued)

Frequency range	Device
174 to 216 MHz	Television stations (channels 7 through 13)
~ 900 MHz, ~ 2.4 GHz, ~ 5 GHz	Cordless phones
1.2276 and 1.57542 GHz	Global Positioning Systems (GPS)

You can get a more detailed frequency allocation chart from *http://www.ntia. doc.gov/osmhome/allochrt.pdf*. The following is a conversion list that should help you understand this chart:

- 1 kiloHertz (kHz) = 1000 Hz
- 1 MegaHertz (MHz) = 1000 kHz
- 1 GigaHertz (GHz) = 1000 MHz

Radio Wave Behavior

Radio waves, like light waves, exhibit certain characteristics when coming into contact with objects. Here are some of the possible behaviors.

Reflection. *Reflection* occurs when a radio wave hits an object that is larger than the wavelength of the radio wave (see Figure 1-9). The radio wave is then reflected off the surface.

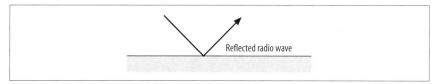

Figure 1-9. Reflection of a radio wave

Refraction. *Refraction* occurs when a radio wave hits an object of a higher density than its current medium (see Figure 1-10). The radio wave now travels at a different angle. An example would be radio waves propagating through clouds.

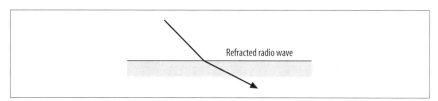

Figure 1-10. Refraction of a radio wave

Scattering. *Scattering* occurs when a radio wave hits an object of irregular shape, usually an object with a rough surface area (see Figure 1-11), and the radio wave bounces off in multiple directions.

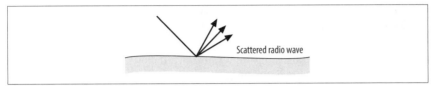

Figure 1-11. Scattering of a radio wave

Absorption. *Absorption* occurs when a radio wave hits an object that does not cause it to be reflected, refracted, or scattered, so it is absorbed by the object (see Figure 1-12). The radio wave is then lost.

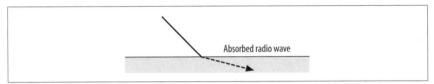

Figure 1-12. Absorption of a radio wave

Radio Interference and Absorption

Radio waves are subject to interference caused by objects and obstacles in the air. Such obstacles can be concrete walls, metal cabinets, or even raindrops. In general, transmissions made at higher frequencies are more subject to radio absorption (by the obstacles) and larger signal loss. Larger frequencies have smaller wavelengths, and hence signals with smaller wavelengths tend to be absorbed by the obstacles that they collide with. This causes high frequency devices to have a shorter operating range.

For devices that transmit data at high frequencies, much more power is needed in order for them to cover the same range as compared to lower frequency transmitting devices.

Diffraction. Sometimes a radio wave will be blocked by objects standing in its path. In this case, the radio wave is broken up and bends around the corners of the object (see Figure 1-13). It is this property that allows radio waves to operate without a visual line of sight.

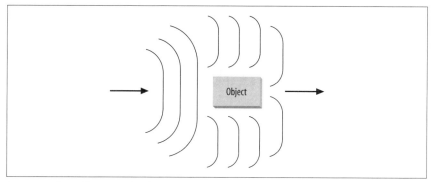

Figure 1-13. Diffraction of radio waves

Wireless Networks

In 1970, the University of Hawaii created a wireless network called ALOHA-NET. Since then, wireless networking has come a long way. ALOHANET operated in the UHF range, and reached 4.8 Kbps, at which speed it could take half an hour to download a 1 MB file. Today, wireless LANs use frequencies of 2.4 GHz and 5 GHz, and can reach speeds (after accounting for network overhead) of 20 Mbps, transferring that 1 MB file in a fraction of a second.

Wi-Fi on Your Notebook

Computer networks have traditionally been Ethernet networks, which use Unshielded Twisted Pair (UTP) cables to wire up all the computers participating in a network. However, as users carry portable computers around (or away from) the office and home, common applications such as email, web browsers, and instant messenger demand network access. Short-range wireless networks can meet the demand for network access without the need for cabling in every place someone might use a computer.

Educational institutions are taking a lead in the adoption of wireless networks, particularly in the classroom environment where students are equipped with a notebook computer and need to move from classroom to classroom while maintaining access to the network. Another area where wireless networking is rapidly gaining ground is among home users. As computers get cheaper and more powerful, it is not uncommon for people to have several computers at home. Wiring up the home is usually undesirable, since it involves costly cable-laying and often destroys the aesthetics of the house. With a wireless network, home users can link up all the computers in the house at an affordable price and without laying a single cable.

Behind the conveniences of accessing the network wirelessly is the IEEE 802.11 standard, a physical layer protocol and a data link layer protocol for wireless communication using radio waves. In this chapter, I lay the foundation for understanding and using a wireless network, so that you can learn how to set up and configure your Windows XP computer for wireless access.

802.11 Wireless Standards

The 802.11 wireless standard is a family of specifications for wireless technology. It was (and is still) developed by the Institute of Electrical and Electronics Engineers (IEEE). 802.11 specifies a client communicating over the air with another client (or through a base station). It comprises the following specifications:

802.11

This is the original specification for wireless networks. The 802.11 standard specifies a transmission rate of 1 or 2 Mbps, and it operates over the 2.4 GHz spectrum. It uses either a Frequency Hopping Spread Spectrum (FHSS) or a Direct Sequence Spread Spectrum (DSSS) modulation scheme.

802.11b

802.11b is more popularly known as Wi-Fi (Wireless Fidelity). This is an extension of the original 802.11 specification. More significantly, 802.11b operates at a much higher data rate, 11 Mbps. However, it can also fall back to a slower rate of 5.5, 2, or 1 Mbps. 802.11b uses only DSSS. Like the original 802.11 standard, 802.11b operates in the 2.4 GHz spectrum. Most wireless networks deployed at the time of this writing are 802.11b networks.

> The term Wi-Fi has now been extended to cover not only 802.11b, but the entire family of 802.11 specifications, such as 802.11a and 802.11g. The Wi-Fi Alliance (*http://www.wi-fi.org/*), a nonprofit organization formed to promote 802.11 wireless technologies, uses the term Wi-Fi to refer to 802.11a, 802.11b, and 802.11g wireless networks.

802.11a

The 802.11a is a relatively new extension to the 802.11 specification. It addresses the slower data rate of the 802.11 and 802.11b specifications by allowing data rates of up to 54 Mbps. It does not use the FHSS or DSSS encoding scheme, but instead uses the Orthogonal Frequency Division Multiplexing (OFDM) modulation scheme. The most significant point about 802.11a is that it is not compatible with the existing 802.11b networks because it operates in the 5 GHz spectrum.

802.11g

The latest addition to the 802.11 family is the 802.11g specification. 802.11g is a competing standard to 802.11a. Similar to 802.11a, 802.11g uses OFDM, but it operates in the 2.4 Ghz spectrum, which is compatible with 802.11b. 802.11g supports up to a maximum of 54 Mbps.

> The data rates specified for 802.11b (11 Mbps) and 802.11a/g (54 Mbps) are raw, and don't reflect what you'll actually experience in everyday use. Because of network overhead, 802.11b users will get between 4 and 5.5 Mbps; 802.11a/g users can expect about 25 Mbps. Further, this is shared between all users of a given base station.

Understanding DSSS and OFDM

DSSS is a transmission technology that transmits data in small pieces over a number of discrete frequencies. Essentially it splits each byte into several bits and sends them on different frequencies. (802.11 uses FHSS, which is similar, but hops across frequencies many times a second.)

OFDM, on the other hand, uses several overlapping frequencies to send packets of data simultaneously. What's more, it splits the overlapping frequencies into smaller frequencies for its own data transmission. Hence, 802.11a and 802.11g can transmit at a higher data rate, since these two standards use OFDM.

The predominant 802.11 specification in use today is 802.11b. With the explosion of network-intensive applications such as streaming video between a computer and Personal Video Recorder (PVR), 802.11b networks are increasingly unable to meet the speed demands of users. Hence network infrastructure designers are looking for faster standards available today and tomorrow. They have to weigh the different criteria when deciding on the suitable specifications to follow. In the next section, you will see a more detailed comparison of the various 802.11 specifications, which will help you make an informed decision.

Comparing 802.11a, 802.11b, and 802.11g

To start off, let's compare 802.11a and the current 802.11b standard by looking at a few parameters. Table 2-1 lists the comparisons sorted according to basic characteristics.

Table 2-1. Comparing 802.11a and 802.11b

	802.11b	802.11a
Modulation and power consumption	802.11b uses the DSSS modulation scheme. In terms of power efficiency, DSSS is more efficient than OFDM.	802.11a uses OFDM. 802.11a devices consume more power than 802.11b devices.
Frequency	802.11b uses the 2.4 GHz spectrum, which is overcrowded with devices such as cordless phones and microwave ovens. Even Bluetooth devices use the 2.4 Ghz spectrum.	802.11a uses the 5 GHz spectrum. Though the 5 GHz spectrum is less crowded, the signals have a higher absorption rate and are easily blocked by walls and objects.

Table 2-1. Comparing 802.11a and 802.11b (continued)

	802.11b	802.11a
Range	802.11b has a range of 300 feet. But this is dependent on the environment. Obstacles such as concrete walls and metal cabinets can reduce the effective range of 802.11b networks.	Due to the higher absorption rate at the 5 GHz spectrum, 802.11a devices have shorter operating range of about 150 feet, compared to the 300 feet achievable by 802.11b (optimally under ideal conditions). As a result, more transmitters are required for 802.11a networks.
Data rate	802.11b supports raw speeds of up to 11 Mbps with a peak speed of 4 to 5.5 Mbps after accounting for network overhead.	802.11a supports raw speeds up to 54 Mbps with a peak speed of approximately 25 Mbps after accounting for network overhead.
Cost	Cost of 802.11b devices have gone down due to the maturity of the 802.11b technologies.	Components for 802.11a devices are more expensive to produce and hence their price tags are higher than 802.11b devices. Also, the increased number of transmitters required for the 802.11a network will drive up the cost of implementing an 802.11a network.
Compatibility	802.11b wireless networks are prevalent, and most current wireless networks use 802.11b devices.	802.11a is not compatible with the 802.11b protocol. Hence 802.11a devices cannot work with existing 802.11b wireless access points (but see the "Dual Band and Compatibility" sidebar later in this chapter). Note that if you plan on migrating to the newer 802.11g standard, your 802.11b cards can still access the "g" network. This will not be the case for 802.11a radio cards.
Users	Supports between 30 and 60 simultaneous wireless users per base station, depending on the device specifications and kind of user activities.	The 802.11a network can accommodate more users (compared to 802.11b) due to the increase in radio frequency channels and increased operating bandwidth.

The main draw of migrating to an 802.11a network is no doubt increased bandwidth. With the near five-fold increase in data rate (54 Mbps), applications like streaming audio and video and networked games would now be possible (or at least more responsive).

Dual Band and Compatibility

The main drawback in adopting 802.11a networks is compatibility. Businesses and institutions that have invested in 802.11b networks are reluctant to migrate to a faster but incompatible 802.11a network. For these reasons, vendors are coming out with dual-band wireless access points and network adapters. These dual-band access points and network adapters contain two sets of hardware, one for 802.11a and one for 802.11b, which let you deploy both 802.11a and 802.11b devices in the same environment. Best of all, since these two protocols operate in different frequencies, interference is minimized.

How about the newer 802.11g standard? How does it compare to 802.11a? Table 2-2 is a comparison of 802.11a and 802.11g standards.

Table 2-2. Comparing 802.11a and 802.11g

	802.11a	802.11g
Modulation and power consumption	Both 802.11a and 802.11g utilize OFDM.	Both 802.11a and 802.11g utilize OFDM, which leads 802.11a and 802.11g to have similar power consumption needs.
Frequency	Uses the 5 GHz spectrum. The number of nonoverlapping channels in 802.11a is eight. The eight nonoverlapping channels in 802.11a make for an increase in throughput (see the section "Channels" later in this chapter).	Unlike 802.11a, 802.11g uses the same 2.4 GHz spectrum as 802.11b. The number of non-overlapping channels in 802.11g is three (see the section "Channels" later in this chapter), compared to eight in 802.11a networks. This makes channel assignment more difficult for 802.11g networks and reduces the effective throughput in a given area.
Range	Both 802.11a and 802.11g have a shorter operating range than 802.11b, due to the higher absorption rate.	See 802.11a column.
Data rate	Both 802.11a and 802.11g support a maximum raw data rate of 54 Mbps, with a peak speed of approximately 25 Mbps after accounting for network overhead.	See 802.11a column.

Table 2-2. Comparing 802.11a and 802.11g (continued)

	802.11a	802.11g
Cost	802.11a and 802.11g networking equipment cost about the same.	802.11g can preserve the current investment in the 802.11b network, allowing you to gradually phase in 802.11g, replacing equipment at whatever pace suits your budget.
Compatibility	802.11a is neither compatible with 802.11g nor 802.11b (see the "Dual Band and Compatibility" sidebar for information about devices that can operate on 802.11b and 802.11a networks).	802.11g allows both 802.11b and 802.11g devices to coexist in the same network.

The question remains: which standard should you go for, 802.11a or 802.11g? The answer depends very much on your environment. Since each offers similar performance in terms of transfer rate, the other criteria that you should consider is your investment in current 802.11b technologies. If preserving compatibility with older equipment is your priority, then 802.11g should be the clear choice. If you are more concerned about pure performance and need to avoid interference with the already crowded 2.4 GHz spectrum, 802.11a would be the recommended route. Another concern is interoperability with equipment from other vendors. For example, Apple has decided not to invest in 802.11a and instead supports 802.11g in its Airport Extreme line of wireless networking equipment. So, an Apple computer or access point would work with 802.11b or 802.11g equipment, but not 802.11a.

 At the time of this writing, D-Link has launched a tri-mode wireless access point (the DI-774) that supports 802.11a, 802.11b, and 802.11g wireless networks.

Wireless Cards and Adapters

Now that we have seen the various wireless standards available in the market, let's turn our attention to the client side of things. Wireless cards and adapters come in the following flavors:

- PCI adapters
- USB adapters
- PCMCIA cards

A PCI wireless adapter is useful for a desktop with an empty PCI slot. Figure 2-1 shows the D-Link DWL-AB520 Multimode Wireless PCI Adapter. It supports both 802.11a and 802.11b wireless standards.

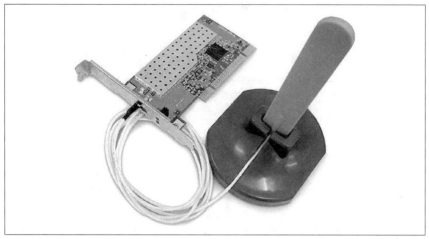

Figure 2-1. The D-Link AirPro DWL-AB520 Multimode Wireless PCI Adapter (802.11a and 802.11b)

If you do not want to open up your computer casing or you simply want to share a wireless adapter among many computers, the Linksys WUSB11 (as shown in Figure 2-2) is a good choice. Simply connect the USB Wireless Adapter to the USB port on your computer and you can get on the wireless network. It supports the 802.11b standard.

Finally, for notebook users, the most popular choice is a PCMCIA card. Figure 2-3 shows the D-Link DWL-G650 wireless card, which supports the 802.11b and 802.11g standards.

Wireless Networking Modes

There are two modes in which your computer can participate in a wireless network. The first, *ad-hoc mode*, is a wireless network where two or more computers communicate with one another directly. It is known as a Basic Service Set (BSS). An ad-hoc network is also known as an Independent Basic Service Set (IBSS). An ad-hoc network does not involve the use of a wireless access point. Each computer on the network communicates with each other in a peer-to-peer fashion. When two or more BSSs operate within the same network, it is then called an Extended Service Set (ESS).

Figure 2-2. The Linksys WUSB11 USB Wireless Adapter (802.11b)

Figure 2-3. The D-Link DWL-G650 AirPlus wireless card (802.11b and 802.11g)

If you want your computer to participate in an ad-hoc network, each computer on the network must have a unique IP address. You can either assign a fixed IP address to your computer or rely on link-local addressing to have your computer automatically assign itself an IP address. See Chapter 5 for information on how to set up an ad-hoc wireless network.

The second mode is infrastructure mode, in which a wireless access point is used. A wireless access point routes the network traffic from one computer to another. It also moves data to the wired network.

Understanding 802.11 Speak

In this section, I discuss some of the terminologies that you will often come across when you set up your wireless network.

WEP

By default, encryption is not enabled for wireless networks. Encryption is important because malicious hackers equipped with the necessary software can sniff the packets transmitted by the wireless network, thereby compromising your data. Wired Equivalent Privacy (WEP) is a protocol used for encrypting packets on a wireless network. It uses a 64-bit (or 256-bit, depending on the equipment) shared key algorithm. Although it is far from perfect, WEP increases the protection of your data, but in doing so reduces your effective data rates.

 Chapter 4 talks about WEP in more detail. More secure techniques used for securing wireless networks such as WPA (Wi-Fi Protected Access) and 802.1X are discussed there.

SSID

The Service Set Identifier (SSID) acts as a name for a wireless network. All devices participating in a particular wireless network must specify this SSID. The wireless devices will not be able to participate in this network if the SSID is not specified (or not stated correctly). For example, Linksys products use the default SSID "linksys" (D-Link products use "default"). If you are concerned about unauthorized users connecting to your access point, you should change this to something else and disable SSID broadcast in the access point's configuration (see Chapter 4). This makes it harder for unauthorized users to find your access point. Use WEP, or if your hardware supports it, 802.1X to allow only authorized users to connect.

Channels

The 802.11b standard defines 14 channels. A *channel* is a particular frequency that is selected so that a Wi-Fi adapter and an access point can communicate at an agreed frequency. Table 2-3 list the frequencies of the 14 channels.

Table 2-3. The frequencies for the 14 channels in 802.11b

Channels	Frequency (GHz)
1	2.412
2	2.417
3	2.422
4	2.427
5	2.432
6	2.437
7	2.442
8	2.447
9	2.452
10	2.457
11	2.462
12	2.467
13	2.472
14	2.484

Not all channels are used universally. In the U.S., only channels 1 to 11 are allowed. In Europe, an additional two channels are allowed, so channels 1 to 13 are usable. In Japan, all fourteen channels are used.

A channel represents the center frequency used by both the radio card and the wireless access point. Each channel occupies 25 MHz of the spectrum (for example, channel 1 ranges from 2.3995 GHz to 2.4245 GHz, a range of 0.025 GHz, or 25 MHz). But this range overlaps with other channels, particularly channels 2 and 3. If you use multiple access points within your network, you need to set the channels of each access point so that they do not overlap, or else they will cause interferences. Figure 2-4 illustrates that the frequency difference between each channel is 5 MHz, but each channel width is 25 MHz. So effectively, to avoid interference, you should use channels 1, 6, and 11 if you are using multiple access points that are within range of each other.

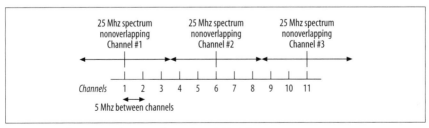

Figure 2-4. The nonoverlapping channels in 802.11b

In infrastructure mode, the access point determines the channel (the access point will come preconfigured to use a particular channel, commonly channel 6); clients are not required to configure the channel number, since they will automatically select the correct channel needed to connect to the access point. For ad-hoc mode, the clients have to select the channel to be used.

In contrast with 802.11b and 802.11g (which has the same three nonoverlapping channels limitation), 802.11a has a total of eight nonoverlapping channels that are 20 MHz wide. Each of these channels is subdivided into 52 subcarriers. And each channel is approximately 300 KHz wide.

Link Quality and Signal Strength

Most access points indicate the link quality and signal strength of a wireless network. *Link quality* is a measure of the ability of the client to communicate with the access point. The signal strength indicator indicates the signals of all received packets. In general, the higher the link quality and signal strength, the better throughput you will get from the wireless network.

MAC Address

In order to uniquely identify each node on the network, every network adapter is assigned a hardware address known as the Media Access Control (MAC) address. This address is assigned by the manufacturer and stored in the card's firmware. A MAC address is a 48-bit number that uniquely identifies a network device. An Ethernet card has a MAC address, as does an 802.11 wireless card. A wireless access point also has a MAC address. For an explanation of how MAC addresses relate to IP addresses, see Chapter 1.

In Windows XP, to find the MAC address of a network device, simply use the ipconfig command:

```
c:\> ipconfig /all
```

You should see something like the following:

```
Ethernet adapter Wireless Network Connection 9:

        Connection-specific DNS Suffix  . : ict.np.edu.sg
        Description . . . . . . . . . . . : Cisco Systems 350 Series
                                            Wireless LAN Adapter
        Physical Address. . . . . . . . . : 00-40-96-40-7E-F9
        Dhcp Enabled. . . . . . . . . . . : Yes
        Autoconfiguration Enabled . . . . : Yes
        IP Address. . . . . . . . . . . . : 192.168.0.197
```

Locking MAC Addresses

Some ISPs use a technique called MAC address locking to prevent unauthorized access to the network. This is how it works: when you subscribe to a broadband service, the ISP will enter the MAC address of your modem into their database. When your modem requests an IP address, the ISP's router checks the MAC address of your modem against its database. If it is not found, no IP address will be issued and you will not be able to get onto the network. Some ISPs also lock the MAC address of your network adapter.

A wireless router has two MAC addresses—one for the local network and one for the WAN (the ISP's network that is connected to the Internet). For those ISPs that lock your network adapter's MAC address, you may have problems in using a wireless router to connect to the Internet. In this case, you can try one of the following:

- In some cases, the MAC address locking is done dynamically. The cable or DSL modem remembers the first MAC address it encounters and won't let any more machines connect unless you reboot it. So, try power-cycling the modem and then doing the same with your access point.

- Give your ISP a call and tell them the MAC address of your wireless access point. Most ISPs are friendly to home networking, but be sure to check the terms of your service agreement before you call.

- Use the Clone MAC address feature, available in most wireless routers, to replace the MAC address of the wireless router with that of the network adapter (whose MAC address is locked by the ISP). All devices connected to the wireless router will now use that particular MAC address to connect to the Internet.

```
Subnet Mask . . . . . . . . . . . : 255.255.255.0
Default Gateway . . . . . . . . . :
DHCP Server . . . . . . . . . . . : 192.168.0.1
DNS Servers . . . . . . . . . . . : 173.21.67.51
                                    173.21.67.52
Lease Obtained. . . . . . . . . . : Wednesday, April 30, 2003
                                    3:05:37 AM

Lease Expires . . . . . . . . . . : Wednesday, May 07, 2003
                                    3:05:37 AM
```

Most wireless cards also have their MAC address printed on the card itself. A typical MAC address looks like this: 00-40-96-40-7E-F9.

Connecting to a Wireless Network

Up to this point, I have discussed the various standards in wireless networks, in particular the IEEE 802.11 specifications. All the theoretical discussions are not very exciting unless you get your hands dirty and try to set up a wireless network yourself. In the following sections, I show you how to connect to a wireless network using three different wireless cards and adapters.

Although I demonstrate each example using different hardware from Cisco, D-Link, and Linksys, wireless hardware vendors use the same or similar chipsets in their equipment. So, the installation and configuration procedures will be somewhat similar across different vendors and different product lines from the same vendor. You should still consult the documentation that comes with your hardware before installing anything.

Most wireless cards in the market today use the following chipsets:

- Atmel
- Broadcom
- Lucent Hermes
- Intersil PRISM-II and Intersil PRISM-2.5
- Symbol Spectrum24
- TI wireless

Some newer 802.11g wireless products (such as those from Linksys) use the Broadcom chipset.

Centrino

Intel's Centrino technology initiative promises smaller laptops with extended battery life and mobile features such as 802.11b networking. For the most part, this means that you're buying a laptop with the Wi-Fi technology embedded deep inside the computer. At the time of this writing, Centrino is 802.11b only, and there is no indication that a Centrino laptop would be upgradeable to 802.11g or 802.11a. So, if you purchase a Centrino laptop, you need to obtain an 802.11a adapter to connect to an 802.11a-only network; you could connect to an 802.11g network, but only at 802.11b speeds. Despite this limitation, a Centrino laptop may be right for you if you're only planning to use 802.11b. For insight on what the bigger picture entails, see Glenn Fleishman's "Centrino: Trojan Horse for Future Cell Data" at *http://wifinetnews.com/archives/001589.html*.

Table 2-4 shows a list of common wireless cards available in the market (all are PC cards unless stated otherwise).

Table 2-4. List of wireless cards and the chipsets used

Card	Chipset
3Com AirConnect 3CRWE737A	Spectrum24
3Com AirConnect 3CRWE777A (PCI)	PRISM-II
Actiontec HWC01170	PRISM-2.5
Actiontec HWC01150	Atmel
Addtron AWP-100	PRISM-II
Agere Orinoco (Lucent)	Hermes
Apple Airport	Hermes
Buffalo AirStation	PRISM-II
Buffalo AirStation (CF)	PRISM-II
Cabletron RoamAbout	Hermes
Compaq Agency NC5004	PRISM-II
Contec FLEXLAN/FX-DS110-PCC	PRISM-II
Corega PCC-11	PRISM-II
Corega PCCA-11	PRISM-II
Corega PCCB-11	PRISM-II
Corega CGWLPCIA11 (PCI)	PRISM-II
D-Link DWL-520 (PCI)	PRISM-2.5
D-Link DWL-650	PRISM-2.5
D-Link DWL-650+	TI Chipset
D-Link DWL-660	TI Chipset
ELSA XI300	PRISM-II
ELSA XI325	PRISM-2.5
ELSA XI325H	PRISM-2.5
ELSA XI800 (CF)	PRISM-II
EMTAC A2424i	PRISM-II
Ericsson Wireless LAN CARD C11	Spectrum24
Gemtek WL-311	PRISM-2.5
Hawking Technology WE110P	PRISM-2.5
I-O DATA WN-B11/PCM	PRISM-II
Intel PRO/Wireless 2011	Spectrum24
Intersil PRISM-II	PRISM-II
Intersil Mini (PCI)	PRISM-2.5
Linksys Instant Wireless WPC11	PRISM-II
Linksys Instant Wireless WPC11 2.5	PRISM-2.5
Linksys Instant Wireless WPC11 3.0	PRISM-2.5

Table 2-4. List of wireless cards and the chipsets used (continued)

Card	Chipset
Lucent WaveLAN	Hermes
Nanospeed ROOT-RZ2000	PRISM-II
NDC/Sohoware NCP130 (PCI)	PRISM-II
NEC CMZ-RT-WP	PRISM-II
Netgear MA401	PRISM-II
Netgear MA401RA	PRISM-2.5
Nokia C020 Wireless LAN	PRISM-I
Nokia C110/C111 Wireless LAN	PRISM-II
NTT-ME 11Mbps Wireless LAN	PRISM-II
Proxim Harmony	PRISM-II
Proxim RangeLAN-DS	PRISM-II
Samsung MagicLAN SWL-2000N	PRISM-II
Symbol Spectrum24	Spectrum24
SMC 2632 EZ Connect	PRISM-II
TDK LAK-CD011WL	PRISM-II
US Robotics 2410	PRISM-II
US Robotics 2445	PRISM-II

I'll start by showing you how to connect to a wireless network. I will illustrate using two wireless cards—the Cisco Aironet 350 and the D-Link DWL-650+, and one USB wireless adapter. I'll take a look at the Cisco Aironet 350 first.

Using a Plug-and-Play PCMCIA Wi-Fi Card

The Cisco Aironet 350 wireless card (see Figure 2-5) is an 802.11b card. This is my preferred card as it is truly plug-and-play—plug this into your PCMCIA slot and Windows XP will connect to the network in seconds! Windows XP includes a driver for this card so there is no need for you to manually install the drivers.

For this section, you need the following:

- A Windows XP notebook computer with a vacant PCMCIA slot
- An existing wireless network (see Chapter 5 for information on setting up a wireless network)
- The Cisco Aironet 350 wireless card

Take the following steps:

1. Insert the Cisco Aironet 350 into your computer's PCMCIA slot.
2. Windows XP will automatically detect the card and install the necessary drivers for it.

Figure 2-5. The Cisco Aironet 350 wireless card

3. Windows XP will then automatically discover any available wireless networks. The Wireless Network Connection icon can be found in the system tray. This is shown in Figure 2-6.

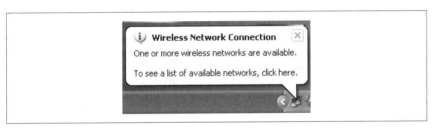

Figure 2-6. The Wireless Network Connection icon in the Tray

4. Click on the Wireless Network Connection icon in the tray to view all
the available wireless networks. Figure 2-7 shows the two available networks with the SSIDs: *MyOffice* and *default*.

5. *MyOffice* has WEP enabled. When you select it, you have to enter a network key. *default* does not have WEP enabled, so when you select it,
you have to turn on the "Allow me to connect to the selected wireless
network, even though it is not secure" option (see Figure 2-8).

6. You can click on the Advanced button to add your own preferred wireless network (see Figure 2-9). This is useful when you use your computer in different places such as home and the office. In the Wireless
Networks tab (see Figure 2-9), there are two sections: Available
networks and Preferred networks. *Available networks* list the SSIDs of
the all wireless networks in range. *Preferred networks* show all the SSIDs
of wireless networks in range plus the networks that you used in the
past. If your wireless network does not broadcast its SSID, you need to
add it manually using the Add button.

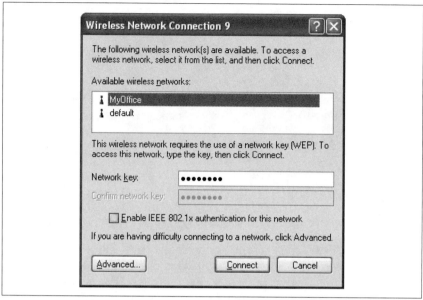

Figure 2-7. Specifying a WEP key for a WEP-secure wireless network

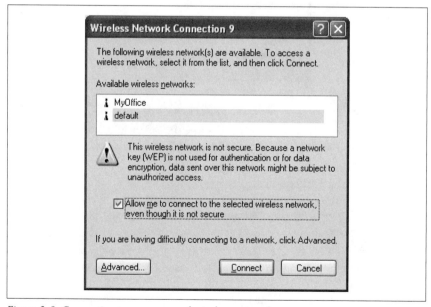

Figure 2-8. Connecting to an unsecured wireless network

To connect to a different wireless network, you can right-click on the Wireless Network Connection icon in the tray and select View Available Wireless Networks (see Figure 2-10).

Windows XP Wireless Zero Configuration

Windows XP provides a Wireless Zero Configuration service. This service is automatically run when your computer is started. You can locate this service in Start → Settings → Control Panel → Administrative Tools → Services.

When the Wireless Zero Configuration service is started, Windows XP will detect the wireless network(s) present and connect to one automatically.

However, if a wireless network has disabled SSID broadcast, Windows XP will not be able to detect the network. In such cases, you need to manually add your wireless network connection (SSID) to the Preferred networks section (click the Advanced button shown in Figures 2-7 and 2-8); Windows XP will automatically connect to the network when it is available again.

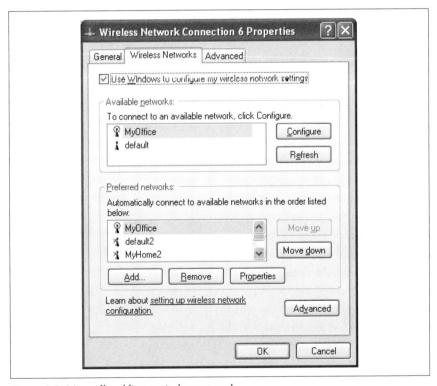

Figure 2-9. Manually adding a wireless network

Using the Cisco Aironet Client Utility (ACU). The Cisco Aironet 350 comes with the Aironet Client Utility (ACU), as shown in Figure 2-11. Strictly speaking, you do not need this for the 350 to work, since Windows XP supports the

Figure 2-10. Windows can automatically display all the available wireless networks

SSID Broadcast and MAC Address Filtering

You will not be able to see the SSID of the network available if the wireless access point has disabled SSID broadcast. To join the network, you need to manually add in the SSID of the network under the Preferred networks section as shown in Figure 2-9.

If the access point uses MAC filtering (and enables SSID broadcast), you would be able to see the SSID of the network but would not be able to connect to it unless your MAC address is in the allow-access list. For information on configuring MAC address filtering, see Chapter 5.

card natively. You can also download the ACU from *http://www.cisco.com/ pcgi-bin/tablebuild.pl/aironet_utilities_windows*.

The ACU comes with an interesting Link Status function that displays the signal strength graphically (see Figure 2-12). This is useful when you need to know where to position yourself so that you get the maximum signal strength for best throughput (see the section "Site Surveys" in Chapter 3).

Using a PCMCIA Wi-Fi Card

The D-Link AirPlus DWL-650+ (see Figure 2-13) is an 802.11b wireless card. When used with another AirPlus product (such as the D-Link AirPlus DI-714P+ wireless router), the maximum raw transfer rate of 22 Mbps can be achieved. For this section, you need the following:

1. A Windows XP notebook computer with a vacant PCMCIA slot
2. An existing wireless network
3. The D-Link AirPlus DWL-650+ wireless card

Using the AirPlus utility. You should download and install the latest driver and utility from D-Link's web site at *http://www.dlink.com/*.

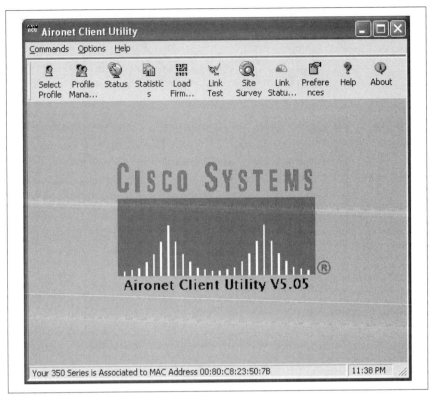

Figure 2-11. The Cisco Aironet Client Utility

To install the DWL-650+, take the following steps:

1. Insert the DWL-650+ into the PCMCIA slot on your computer.
2. Windows XP will detect the presence of the card and search for a suitable driver.
3. If prompted for a driver, direct Windows XP to the drivers that you downloaded.

After the installation, the AirPlus utility icon should appear in the Tray, as shown in Figure 2-14 (the icon in the middle).

Double-click on the icon and the D-Link AirPlus utility window (see Figure 2-15) will appear.

The AirPlus utility contains five main pages:

Link Info
    Displays information about the current connection. Displays the link quality, signal strength, and data rate graphically.

Configuration
    Allows configuration of the current wireless connection.

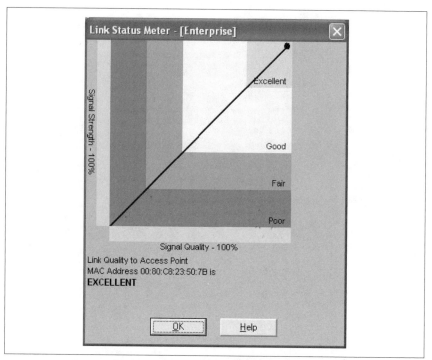

Figure 2-12. The ACU displays the signal strength graphically

Figure 2-13. The D-Link DWL-650+ 802.11b wireless card

Encryption

Specifies whether encryption is used for the wireless network. Also allows you to enter the key(s) used.

SiteSurvey

Displays the available wireless network as well as allows you to manually add networks (see Figure 2-16).

Known Conflicts Between Windows XP and the D-Link DWL-650+

In my testing, the DWL-650+ sometimes conflicts with Windows XP. The AirPlus utility may connect you to a particular network, but after a while, Windows XP will automatically connect to another network, or the network may simply be disconnected.

To solve this problem, disable the wireless zero configuration feature in Windows XP:

1. Go to Start → Settings → Control Panel.
2. Double click on Administrative Tools → Services.
3. Locate the item Wireless Zero Configuration and double-click on it.
4. Click the Stop button to stop the service (you should also change the Startup type to Manual so that the service will not be started the next time your computer reboots).

Once the Windows wireless zero configuration feature is turned off, the DWL-650+ should work perfectly.

In general, if you encounter difficulties connecting to a wireless network, turn off Windows wireless zero configuration and use the utility provided by the wireless card vendor.

Note that when you disable the Windows XP Wireless Zero Configuration service, you lose many of the advanced wireless features found in Windows XP. These include:

- Notification messages such as "One or more wireless networks are available" (Figure 2-6)
- The Wireless Network Connection dialog box (Figure 2-8)
- The Wireless Networks tab of the network connection properties (Figure 2-9)

If you disable this service, you will need to use the configuration utility supplied by your wireless card vendor to connect to a wireless network.

Figure 2-14. The AirPlus utility icon in the Tray

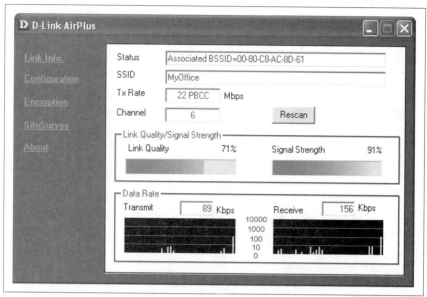

Figure 2-15. Using the D-Link AirPlus utility

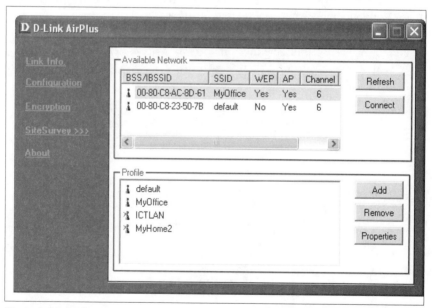

Figure 2-16. Performing a site survey using the D-Link AirPlus utility

Third-party tools like NetStumbler can also assist in doing a wireless site survey. Chapters 3 and 9 discuss NetStumbler in more detail.

About

Displays copyright information and the firmware and utility version numbers.

AirPlus Technology

The D-Link AirPlus product family uses the Texas Instruments' patented Digital Signal Processing technology for enhanced performance. When two products from the AirPlus family are used, it results in improved performance. However, the AirPlus family is also fully compatible with the 802.11b specification and thus will work with all other 802.11b products.

Figure 2-16 shows the result of a site survey. Two wireless networks are detected. When a wireless network with WEP enabled is selected, you are prompted to enter a key, as shown in Figure 2-17.

Using a USB Wi-Fi Adapter

The USB wireless adapter that I use in this section is the Linksys WUSB11 wireless adapter (see Figure 2-2, earlier in this chapter). The benefit of using a USB wireless adapter is that you can use it on your desktop PC as well as on a notebook. It is a useful alternative when you need to share an adapter among multiple computers.

To use the WUSB11, simply connect it to your USB port on your computer and Windows XP will prompt you for the drivers. You should use the drivers provided by Linksys or download them from Linksys's web site at *http://www.linksys.com/*.

Using the Linksys wireless configuration utility. Linksys provides the WUSB11 with a configuration utility. (See Figure 2-18: the utility is represented by a little green icon on the lower right corner. When the network is not present, the icon turns red.)

Using this configuration utility, you can perform a site survey and view the current link quality and signal strength.

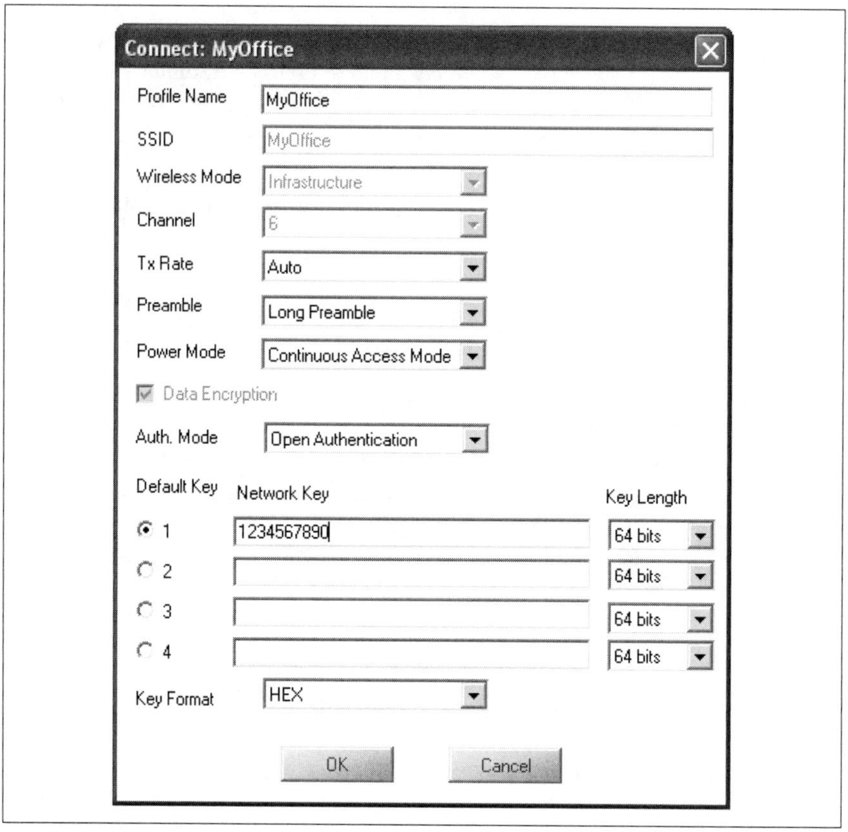

Figure 2-17. Entering a WEP key

Taking It on the Road

Now that you have a better understanding of wireless networks and how you can connect to one using your wireless card or adapter, the following chapter discusses how you can find connectivity while on the road. For information on using Wi-Fi securely, see Chapter 4.

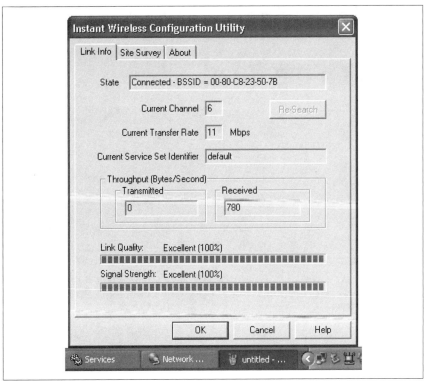

Figure 2-18. The Linksys configuration utility

CHAPTER THREE

Wi-Fi on the Road

If you set up a wireless network in your home or office, you'll probably spend most of your time on that network. However, when you wander away, your wireless adapter will let you access other networks, so why not take advantage of this? For example, you may be traveling and need to get online at the airport or hotel. In this case, you could connect to a commercial or community wireless network (or a cellular network, as described in Chapter 8).

In this chapter, I discuss some of the commercial and community wireless access providers and how you can use them while on the road. I also show you how to hunt for wireless networks using your existing hardware and some free software. This can come in handy when your travel involves a conference, since many conference organizers have begun to include free Wi-Fi as an added feature for attendees.

Wireless Hotspots

As more users equip their portable computers with Wi-Fi, opportunities have emerged for anyone who can bring a DSL line and access point into a public space such as a coffee shop, airport, or public library. Some people will set up an access point and charge by the hour; others will charge nothing, just to attract customers or keep them a little longer; some, such as a library, will set it up to make information more accessible. A venue with this kind of public access point is known as a *wireless hotspot*. The number of wireless hotspots is growing rapidly. Today, you can easily find wireless hotspots in hotels, airports, coffee shops, and metropolitan areas.

In order to see striking views of wireless hotspots in New York City, see the Public Internet Project's maps at *http://publicinternetproject.org/research/moremaps.html*. Chapter 9 includes instructions for generating your own such maps.

If you want to know out whether a particular area has a wireless hotspot, you can search for one at the following web sites:

WiFinder
 http://www.wifinder.com/search.php

HotSpotList
 http://www.hotspotlist.com/

T-Mobile Hotspots
 http://www.t-mobile.com/hotspot/

Wi-Fi Zone Finder
 http://www.wi-fizone.org/zoneLocator.asp

In the following sections, I discuss some of the wireless hotspots provided by commercial service providers as well as end users and community groups.

Wireless Internet Service Providers

Like the conventional Internet Service Provider (ISP), a Wireless Internet Service Provider (WISP) provides Internet access, albeit wirelessly (from the client to the access point). These providers ranges from the big names, such as T-Mobile, WayPort, and Surf and Sip, to the independent wireless operators found in your neighborhood coffee houses and bars.

When you connect to a WISP's hotspot, the first thing you should do is open up a web browser and try to visit a site outside the WISP's network, such as *www.oreilly.com*. This is because many WISPs divert all web traffic to a sign-on page called a captive portal (see Figure 3-1). Until you sign up for the service and pay with your credit card, your access is limited to the captive portal and possibly some portions of the WISP's own web site.

T-Mobile HotSpot. T-Mobile HotSpot (*http://www.t-mobile.com/hotspot/*) is one of the wireless service providers in the U.S. It has coverage in over 2,000 locations such as airports, Starbucks Coffee, and Borders bookstores.

Each location is equipped with a T1 line, providing speedy access to the Internet. The pricing plan is flexible—you can either sign up for an unlimited monthly subscription plan that starts at $29.95 or pay as you go for 10 cents per minute.

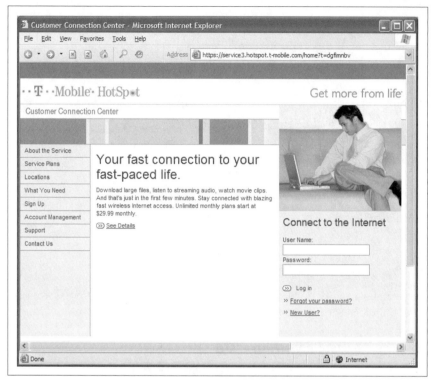

Figure 3-1. T-Mobile's captive portal

You can download a list of T-Mobile Hotspots at *http://locations.hotspot.t-mobile.com/pals.pdf.*

The SSID for the T-Mobile Hotspot is "tmobile."

Surf and Sip. Surf and Sip (*http://www.surfandsip.com/*) provides high-speed Internet access at locations such as cafes, hotels, restaurants, and other public places. Surf and Sip has flexible service plans ranging from monthly subscription to pay-as-you-go pricing.

The SSID for the Surf and Sip wireless network is "SurfandSip."

If you run a business, you can also collaborate with Surf and Sip to offer wireless Internet access at your business location. Surf and Sip will provide all the technology and materials needed and best of all, you get a cut of the revenue generated.

WayPort. WayPort has very good coverage in major hotels (such as the Four Seasons, Loews, Sheraton, Radisson, Hilton, Marriott, Embassy Suites, and Wyndham) and airports (including Dallas/Fort Worth, Atlanta Hartsfield, Chicago O'Hare, New York LaGuardia, Seattle-Tacoma, San Jose, and more) in the U.S. For a list of all WayPort wireless hotspot locations, visit *http://www.wayport.com/locations*.

With so many WISPs offering wireless Internet access, how do you identify one? The easiest way is to look for a sign or logo in the coffee shop or airport. Figure 3-2 shows the signage of T-Mobile, Surf and Sip, and WayPort.

Figure 3-2. The signage of the various WISPs

Which WISP?

So with so many WISPs vying for your attention, which one should you sign up with? Here are some suggestions:

- If you are a frequent traveler, WayPort is a good choice. WayPort covers more airports and hotels in the U.S. than any other WISP.
- If you frequently hang out in places such as Borders or Starbucks Coffee, then T-Mobile is a great choice. T-Mobile has covered many Starbucks and Borders stores in the U.S.
- If T-Mobile is not available at your favorite coffee house, then Surf and Sip might be another viable alternative.
- Many WISPs offer short-term rates that you can sign up for from their captive portal. Since this doesn't involve a long-term commitment, you may find it more convenient to simply pay as you go.

Since Boingo Wireless partners with T-Mobile, WayPort, and Surf and Sip, as well as many other hotspot operators, you can sign up for their service and get access to most, if not all, of the wireless networks you might encounter for a single price. (See the section "Wireless Aggregators" in this chapter.)

Wireless Aggregators

With the proliferation of WISPs and hotspot operators, interoperability becomes crucial. You want to be able to connect wirelessly whenever there is a wireless hotspot, regardless of the WISP that is providing the network.

A *wireless network aggregator* provides uniform access to all the different operators that partner with the aggregator. It is like roaming on your mobile phone, except without the exorbitant fees. Instead of expecting you to sign up with all the phone companies in the countries that you visit, your local phone company works with operators from different countries to provide telephone service outside of your phone company's service areas.

Boingo.com is a wireless network aggregator. Boingo provides several price plans starting from $7.95 for two Connect days (a *Connect day* is 24 hours of unlimited usage per location, starting from the moment you first connect) to $49.95 for monthly unlimited usage.

Using Boingo's software, you can configure your computer to wirelessly connect to the nearest hotspot. As a user, you are shielded from the intricacies of locating the right network and remembering various usernames and passwords.

You can search for over 1,300 hotspots covering 300 cities and 43 states at *http://www.boingo.com/search.html*.

Figure 3-3 shows the Boingo software finding two wireless networks in your immediate vicinity.

Wireless Community Networks

When I first visited the U.S. many years ago, I came across one interesting fact. I realized that in most places it is difficult to find a public washroom—you can usually find one in restaurants or big shopping malls only. Back in Singapore, washrooms are easy to find, and access to most of them is free. Think about it—you pay for water at home, but in public washrooms, it is free (at least to you). If you apply this economic model to Internet access, why not have free Internet access in public places?

The idea that I have to pay for Internet access while I am on the road (or even sipping my coffee at a coffee house) still baffles me. The coffee house *should* provide free Internet access, just like using the water in the washroom is free. Commercial DSL can be had for well under $100 a month in many parts of the United States, and an access point is a one-time expense of under $100. So why not simply use free Wi-Fi as a way to lure customers? Fortunately, many people think likewise and set up free hotspots in their businesses. Some grassroots groups take this a few steps further and form *wireless community networks*.

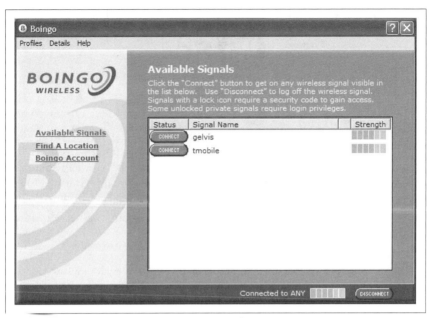

Figure 3-3. Boingo's software locating two networks

Wi-Fi Zone

With so many wireless operators rolling out wireless hotspots, how can you be assured of quality? The Wi-Fi Zone attempts to address this concern.

The Wi-Fi Zone (*http://www.wifizone.org/*) is set up by the Wi-Fi Alliance, a nonprofit international association formed in 1999 to certify interoperability of wireless Local Area Network products based on the IEEE 802.11 specification.

The aim of the Wi-Fi Zone is to establish guidelines for maintaining consistent and dependable wireless access services. Wireless operators who are awarded the Wi-Fi Zone logo have demonstrated their adherence to minimum standards specified by the Wi-Fi Zone, assuring users a first-rate Wi-Fi connection to the Internet.

Visit the following URL for a list of Wi-Fi Zones:

http://www.wifizone.org/zoneLocator.asp

You can also locate a Wi-Fi Zone location by identifying the Wi-Fi Zone logo shown in Figure 3-4.

Figure 3-4. The Wi-Fi Zone logo

The concept of a wireless community network is simple. If you have a broadband connection to the Internet, why not share it? You can share the connection by connecting it to an access point and allowing your neighbors to connect to it as well. If many people do this, coordinate their efforts, and provide a central location where users can learn about the service, it's a community network.

 Refer to *Building Wireless Community Networks*, by Rob Flick-enger (O'Reilly), for a more detailed discussion of community wireless networks.

You find the various wireless communities that are out there by visiting the WirelessCommunities site at *http://www.personaltelco.net/index.cgi/WirelessCommunities*.

Sharing Bandwidth

If you often travel in groups and want to minimize the cost of getting online, bring a wireless access router along with you the next time you travel. The NetGear MR814 802.11b Cable/DSL Wireless Router is a good choice due to its slim design (see Figure 3-5).

Figure 3-5. The NetGear MR814 802.11b Cable/DSL Wireless Router

Instead of connecting your notebook computer directly to a hotel's broad-band connection, connect your wireless router to it and share it wirelessly with your colleagues. This way, all of your traveling companions can access the network at the same time.

If you don't feel like carrying a router with you when you travel, you can also share a connection using an ad-hoc network (see Chapter 5).

Finding Wireless Networks

Finding commercial wireless operators is easy—very often you can identify the signage hanging outside a coffee house or on the walls of a hotel lobby. If not, when you power up your Windows XP computer equipped with a wireless card, it will display a list of wireless networks available. Examining the SSIDs (see Chapter 2 for more information on SSIDs) will often allow you to identify the network operator instantly.

This section focuses on how you can locate wireless networks when on the road. It is useful as a guide to help you look out for wireless networks in places such as hotels, coffee houses, or libraries.

Site Surveys

A simple way to discover wireless networks is to perform a site survey with your wireless network card. Doing a site survey is simple using either Windows XP's built-in capabilities or an advanced tool such as NetStumbler.

Check out the utility software bundled with your wireless card. Very often it comes with an application that allows you to perform site surveys.

Windows XP. Windows XP's Wireless Zero Configuration feature automatically discovers the available wireless networks in the vicinity (this feature was illustrated in Chapter 2). However, Windows XP does not allow you to see detailed information about the wireless networks, such as the number of access points available or where they are located. If you need the additional information, you should use the more sophisticated (and free) NetStumbler program.

NetStumbler. NetStumbler is a free wireless network discovery tool (written by Marius Miner, a San Francisco Bay area software developer) that runs on Windows-based computers. You can use NetStumbler for site surveys, and it is also a useful tool for detecting unauthorized (rogue) access points.

Check out NetStumbler's web site to see if your wireless card is supported. NetStumbler generally works with wireless cards using the Hermes chipset (refer to Chapter 2 for a list of wireless cards using the Hermes chipset). However, some cards that are not supported by NetStumbler (such as those from Cisco and D-Link) work under Windows XP. My Cisco Aironet 350 works well with NetStumbler.

You can download NetStumbler from *http://www.netstumbler.com/*. Running NetStumbler will display a list of wireless access points detected.

As shown in Figure 3-6, NetStumbler groups the access points detected based on channels and SSIDs. In this case, several access points were found running on channel 6. The MAC addresses of the access point are also displayed, together with other information such as vendor of the access point, whether WEP was used, signal-to-noise ratio, etc.

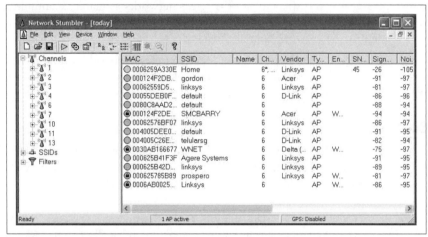

Figure 3-6. Using NetStumbler to detect wireless networks

 If you do a site survey using NetStumbler and find a bunch of access points, you may be surprised to see the number of wireless networks that do not use any kind of security.

NetStumbler also includes GPS support so you can connect a GPS receiver to your notebook and collect the location information for all the access points you find. Feeding the latitude and longitude information to mapping software (such as Microsoft MapPoint) lets you plot a map showing the locations of the access points. See Chapter 9 for more details on how to use NetStumbler with GPS.

Determining wireless coverage with NetStumbler. You can use NetStumbler to display a graph depicting the signal-to-noise ratio of a given access point (see Figure 3-7). This is useful for helping network administrators select the best place to position an access point for maximum coverage.

Wardriving, Warwalking, and Warflying

A new term has been coined to describe the act of doing site surveys: *Wardriving*. Wardriving involves people using their notebook computers or Pocket PCs (equipped with wireless cards and GPS receivers) and driving around the city (or neighborhood) looking for the presence of wireless networks—just for the fun or it, or to assess the security risks of wireless networks. With a GPS receiver, wardrivers can catalog the exact location of an access point. Besides Wardriving, people who performed site surveys via walking are Warwalking. Well, *Warflying* then seems obvious—you fly on an airplane doing site surveys (for a great Warflying story, see Philip Windley's weblog at *http://www.windley.com/2002/09/02.html*).

To see the Wardriving efforts around the world, go to *google.com* and type in "Wardriving".

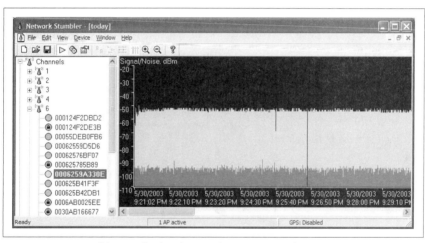

Figure 3-7. NetStumbler can display the signal-to-noise ratio for an access point.

NetStumbler displays the graph in two colors: green and red. If the graph displays in mostly green, then it means that the signal quality is good. In general, always aim for lots of green in your graph.

To aim for maximum coverage, once an access point is mounted, install NetStumbler on a notebook computer and call up the graph. (To view this graph, drill down into the list of channels or SSIDs on the left and locate the access point you're interested in.) Watch the graph for a few seconds, and you'll see that it is charting the signal-to-noise ratio over time. So, if you walk around the site you wish to survey, you'll see the values change as the quality of coverage increases or decreases.

Is Wardriving Legal?

Before you do your own Wardriving, be sure to check with the local authorities to see if it is legal. As far as I know, Wardriving is not illegal in the U.S. However, in some countries, Wardriving may be an offense (in Singapore, it is classified under the Computer Misuse Act).

One way to protect yourself when doing a Wardrive is to disable DHCP on your computer. Set a static IP address for your computer so that when you are associated with an access point, the network does not assign an IP address to you. Technically speaking, so long as you have not been assigned an IP address by the wireless network (even though you have been associated with the access point), you have not joined the network, and so you cannot be held liable for trespassing into the network.

However, if you use DHCP for IP address, and an IP address is assigned to you, your MAC address will be logged by the network. Depending on local law, this may make you liable for your action.

Warchalking

Warchalking is the practice of drawing symbols on walls to indicate a nearby wireless network. With the symbols, wireless users can identify the areas in which they can connect wirelessly to the Internet. Figure 3-8 shows the symbols used for Warchalking. The web site for Warchalking can be found at *http://www.warchalking.org/*.

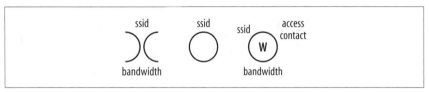

Figure 3-8. Symbols used for Warchalking (from left to right: an open network, a closed network, and a network protected by WEP)

How Warchalking came about. In the 1930s during the Great Depression, many people left their homes to look elsewhere for jobs. Due to the poverty and scarcity of work, everywhere these people (often known as hobos) were often unwelcome in the new cities. As the story goes, a group flocked to Texas because it was rumored that there was a town there called El Paso where people were generous to beggars. To avoid trouble with the locals, the hobos devised a set of symbols to communicate with each other, so that they knew what to expect in the unfamiliar town. Figure 3-9 shows some original symbols devised by the hobos. Can you figure out what they mean?

Figure 3-9. Some symbols used by the hobos

Here are the answers:

1. You will be beaten
2. Man with gun
3. Safe camp

You can visit the following web sites for more symbols used by the hobos:

- *http://www.slackaction.com/signroll.htm*
- *http://sedaliakatydepot.com/hobo.htm*

Matt Jones, an Internet product designer, operates a web site (*http://blackbeltjones.com*) that serves primarily as the Londoner's online resume and portfolio. In June 2002, Jones combined the practice of using a sniffer tool to detect a wireless network (known as Wardriving or Warwalking) with that of the hobos' symbol to come up with the symbols for wireless networks (see Figure 3-8). Using these symbols, wireless users can then know if there is an available wireless network for their use. He was inspired by architecture students "chalking up the pavement" on his way to lunch. During a lunch, Jones and a friend, who had recently been discussing hobo signs with another friend, came up with the notion of Warchalking.

So the next time you see such a symbol on a wall or a sidewalk, you know that there is probably wireless access in the vicinity. Once you know about it, what can you do with it? To answer this question, you need to consider the legal and moral aspects of Warchalking.

Warchalking, Wardriving, and Legality

Warchalking or Wardriving for wireless networks are activities that are still legally debatable at the moment. First, drawing chalk marks on the wall may not constitute an offense (this depends on where you live: it is definitely considered an offense in Singapore if you do it without explicit permission!). But the real concern is when you discover a wireless network in a nearby home or business. Unlike wired networks, a wireless network has no clear boundary; hence, how does one define trespassing?

What happens if a wireless home network is not protected by any form of security (see Chapter 4) or MAC address filtering (see Chapter 5)? In this case, the wireless network is deemed to be "open" and may suggest that strangers are welcome to use the network. So, should you connect to the network? There is no clear answer.

At the time of this writing, a bill (House Bill 495) is moving through the New Hampshire state legislature that defines explicit boundaries for this. Under this bill, users would effectively be permitted to connect to open wireless networks. House Bill 495 recognizes that an open network is often a welcome mat. After all, if you were sitting in a public place such as a hotel lobby, airport, coffee shop, library, or conference venue and found an open access point, what would your first instinct be? Would you connect to the wireless network or find someone in order to ask permission? Most users would assume that the network was put there for their use. If passed, House Bill 495 would still protect wireless network operators by requiring them to take some steps to secure their network in order to be able to prosecute unauthorized users who connect to their network. If this sort of legislation becomes more common, then the legality of Warchalking and Wardriving will be easier to evaluate on a case-by-case basis.

Communicating Securely

With no physical boundary, how can wireless networks be secure? Can they be locked down sufficiently to please security-conscious users? Because the initial wireless security standard was fundamentally flawed, the answer is complicated. In this chapter, I explain the security issues inherent in the 802.11 family and the various ways you can secure a wireless network.

Secure Wireless Computing

Before we start discussing the gory details of Wi-Fi LAN security, let me make one thing clear: Wired Equivalent Privacy (WEP), the security protocol used by most 802.11 networks at the time of this writing, is fundamentally flawed. Though I talk about WEP in much more detail later in this chapter, here is a quick rundown of WEP's flaws:

- All users in a wireless network share the same secret key. (And a secret key is no longer a secret if more than one person knows it.)

- The implementation of WEP makes it very susceptible to attacks by hackers. It is not a matter of whether it can be cracked, but a matter of how soon. The flaws in WEP have been proven both in theory and practice.

Although WEP has its flaws, it's worth using to discourage unauthorized users from connecting to your access point. If you need stronger security, you have to rely on other techniques to provide it. In the first part of this chapter, I assume that you are connected to a wireless network (with or without WEP), and that you want to securely access the network resources (including something as simple as surfing the Web or reading your email). I discuss three ways in which you can have more secure wireless communications in the list shown next.

Virtual Private Networks (VPN)

A VPN allows you to remotely access a private network as though you were connected to it physically. Moreover, the entire communication channel is protected by encryption. So if you are connected to a VPN server wirelessly, the packets transmitted between your computer and the access point are encrypted by the VPN connection, which is much more secure than using WEP.

Secure Shell (SSH)

SSH lets you initiate a shell session (similar to Telnet) or exchange files with a remote server, with the information exchanges all encrypted. When not using a VPN, SSH is an excellent option for securely connecting to another computer.

Firewalls

If you connect to public networks where your fellow users are unknown and untrusted, a good firewall can provide some degree of security. Windows XP includes basic firewall capabilities; there are third-party firewall applications available that have more features.

After this, I go into the details of Wi-Fi security and the various technologies that are in use (or have been proposed) for securing wireless networks.

Virtual Private Networks

Imagine you are out of the office and need to access a printer or file server on the office network. Unless you dial in to the company's server, it is not possible for you to access the resources in the office. Moreover, using a dial-up line is not a cheap alternative (despite the slow speed), especially if you are overseas.

A Virtual Private Network (VPN) allows you to establish a secure, encrypted connection to the office's network, all through a public network such as the Internet. Using a VPN, you can work as though you are connected to your company's network.

There are two main types of VPN:

User-to-Network

This type allows a client to use a VPN to connect to a secure network, such as a corporate intranet.

Network-to-Network

This type connects two networks via a VPN connection. This effectively combines two disparate networks into one, eliminating the need for a Wide Area Network (WAN).

Tunneling

Tunneling is the process of encapsulating packets within other packets to protect their integrity and privacy during transit. A tunnel performs such tasks as encryption, authentication, packet forwarding, and masking of IP private addresses. Figure 4-1 shows a tunnel established between two computers through the Internet. Think of a tunnel as a private link between the two computers: whatever one sends to another is only visible to the other, even though it is sent through a public network like the Internet.

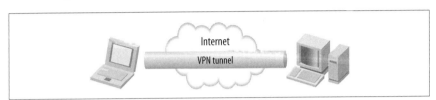

Figure 4-1. A tunnel established between two computers in a VPN

The following section discusses some tunneling protocols available for VPNs.

PPTP, L2TP, and IPSec. If you're curious about what goes on under the hood of a VPN, there are three protocols that you need to know: PPTP, L2TP, and IPSec:

Point-to-Point Tunneling Protocol (PPTP)
> This was designed by Microsoft (and other companies) to create a secure tunnel between two computers. PPTP provides authentication and encryption services, and encapsulates PPP packets within IP packets. It supports multiple Microsoft networking protocols such as LAN to LAN and dial-up connections. However, it is proprietary and the encryption is weak.

Layer 2 Tunneling Protocol (L2TP)
> This works like PPTP, except that it does not include encryption. L2TP was proposed by Cisco Systems, and like PPTP, supports multiple networking protocols.

IPSec
> This addresses the shortcomings of L2TP by providing encryption and authentication of IP packets. As such, L2TP is often used together with IPSec to provide a secure connection.

> If possible, a VPN should be used together with 802.1X. 802.1X adds an additional layer of protection that the VPN itself does not possess. For more information on VPNs, see *Virtual Private Networks* (O'Reilly).

Setting Up a VPN Connection Between Two Computers

In the following sections, I illustrate how to set up a VPN host as well as a client using two Windows XP Professional systems.

On the host computer. Let's start with setting up the VPN host:

1. On the desktop, right-click on Network Connections.
2. Select "Create a new connection".
3. In the New Connection Wizard window, select "Set up an advanced connection" (see Figure 4-2). Click Next.

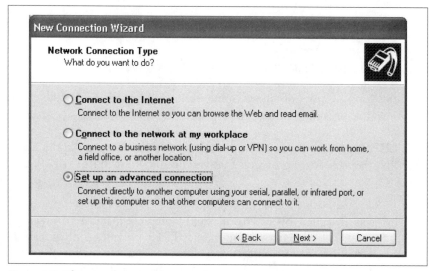

Figure 4-2. Choosing the network connection type

4. Select "Accept incoming connections". Click Next.
5. In the next window, you can select the other devices to accept the incoming connection. Click Next.
6. Select "Allow virtual private connections" and click Next (see Figure 4-3).
7. Select the users that you want to allow to connect to your computer using the VPN connection (see Figure 4-4). Click Next.
8. The next window allows you to install additional networking software for this connection (see Figure 4-5). Click on Next to go to the next screen.
9. Click on Next and then Finish to complete the process.

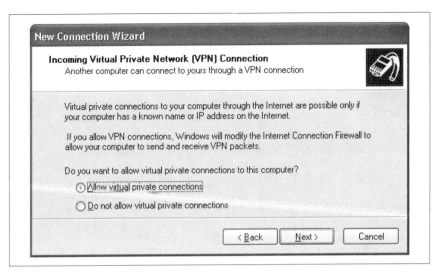

Figure 4-3. Allowing a VPN connection

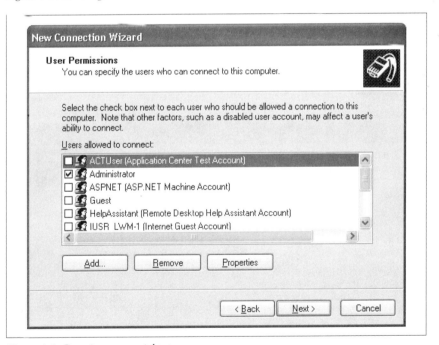

Figure 4-4. Granting access rights to users

On the client. To configure Windows XP to connect to a VPN:

1. On the desktop, right-click on Network Connections.

2. Select "Create a new connection".

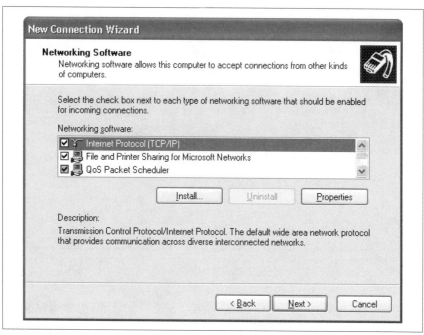

Figure 4-5. Installing the networking software for the VPN connection

3. Select "Connect to the network at my workplace" (see Figure 4-6).

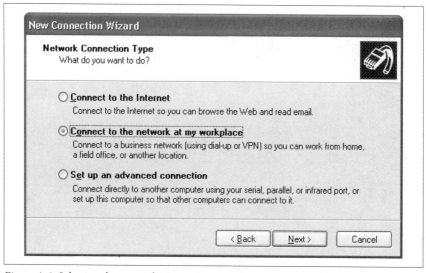

Figure 4-6. Selecting the network connection type

4. Select "Virtual Private Network connection" (see Figure 4-7). Click Next.

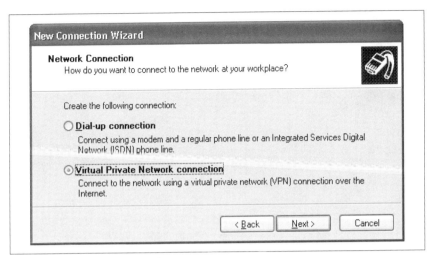

Figure 4-7. Selecting the network connection

5. Enter a name for the VPN connection (see Figure 4-8). Click Next.

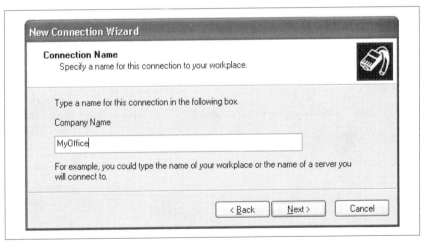

Figure 4-8. Giving your VPN connection a name

6. Select "Do not dial the initial connection". Click Next.

7. Enter the IP address of the VPN server (see Figure 4-9). Click Next.

8. Select "My use only" (see Figure 4-10). Click Next.

9. Turn on the "Add a shortcut to this connection to my desktop" checkbox. Click Finish.

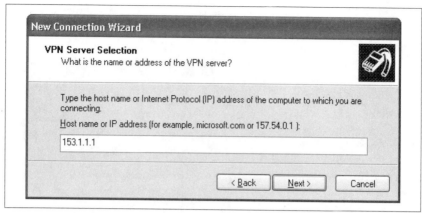

Figure 4-9. Specifying the IP address of the VPN host

Figure 4-10. Setting the connection availability

That's it! When the process is completed, an icon is shown on the desktop (see Figure 4-11).

MyOffice

Figure 4-11. The icon for the VPN connection

To connect to the VPN server, double-click on the icon and log in with your username information (see Figure 4-12). You can now work as though you are working on a computer in your office: most (if not all) of your network resources, such as file and print servers, will be accessible.

Resist the temptation to check the box titled "Save this user name and password for the following users" (see Figure 4-12). If you enable this, your password will be saved on your computer; if your computer is stolen or compromised, an attacker will be able to connect to the VPN and access everything it protects.

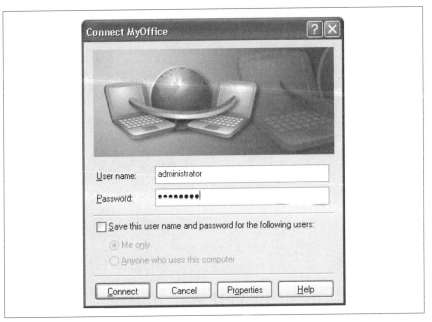

Figure 4-12. Logging in to a VPN connection

One common error that you might encounter has to do with setting a proxy server in Internet Explorer. For example, my ISP does not require me to use a proxy server when surfing the Web. But when I connected to the VPN server in my workplace, I was suddenly unable to connect to the Web. As it turns out, my company requires me to use a proxy server to connect to the Web. With the proxy server configured in IE (Tools → Internet Options → Connections → Connection Name → Settings), I am now able to connect to the Web (see Figure 4-13).

Secure Shell (SSH)

If you need to connect to Unix or Linux servers, you may be familiar with utilities such as *Telnet* and *FTP*. Telnet lets you connect to a command

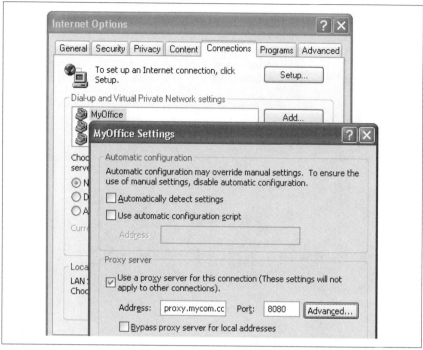

Figure 4-13. Setting a proxy server for a VPN connection

IPSec and PPTP Pass Through

Most wireless routers support a feature known as "IPSec and PPTP pass through." What does it do?

IPSec and PPTP are security protocols that provide authentication and encryption over the Internet. The "pass through" feature of the wireless router allows secure packets to flow through the router, but the router itself does not perform any authentication and encryption operation.

IPSec works in two modes: transport and tunnel. Transport mode secures IP packets from source to destination, whereas tunnel mode puts an IP packet into another packet that is sent to the tunnel's endpoint. Only tunnel mode (ESP) IPSec can be passed through.

prompt on a machine over the network. The FTP utility transfers files between your machine and a remote server.

If you are using either Telnet or FTP to connect to a sensitive server, but you're not also using a VPN, you are probably exposing your password to anyone who can access the network you're connected to (perhaps you're on a public network at a wireless hotspot?), the network where the remote server resides, and any network in between. (Ever wonder what networks sit between you and a remote computer? Use the tracert command at the Windows XP Command Prompt to trace the route between your computer and a remote host, as in tracert www.oreilly.com).

 Anonymous FTP, in which you use your email address as a password, is not a concern. This is because, as the name implies, all remote users are treated as anonymous guests, and, if the remote FTP server is configured properly, are accorded no privileges that could be abused.

If the remote server supports it, you can use the Secure Shell (SSH) protocol to work with a remote machine's command prompt (replacing Telnet) or securely transfer files (replacing FTP). SSH Communications Security offers SSH utilities for Windows and other platforms. Open source variants include *openssh* (*http://www.openssh.org*), which is included with the Cygwin (*http://www.cygwin.com*) distribution, a Linux-like environment for Windows. However, since Cygwin has a fairly big footprint, a popular open source alternative is PuTTY, a suite of SSH utilities that fit on a floppy disk.

PuTTY is available from *http://www.chiark.greenend.org.uk/~sgtatham/putty/*. At a minimum, you should download and install (put the *.exe* somewhere in your Windows PATH) *putty.exe*. If you want to perform secure file transfers, download *pscp.exe* and *psftp.exe*.

To connect to a remote host with PuTTY, launch the application, specify SSH as the protocol (the default is to use the insecure Telnet protocol), and supply the IP address or hostname of the machine to which you want to connect, as shown in Figure 4-14.

The first time you connect to a remote server with PuTTY, it will advise you that the server is unknown to it (see Figure 4-15). Click Yes or No to continue connecting, and then type your username and password when prompted to do so.

Once you are logged in, you can issue commands on the remote machine as shown in Figure 4-16.

You can use *pscp* (secure copy) and *psftp* (secure FTP) at the Windows XP Command Prompt. To copy a file with *pscp*, use pscp *username@host:path*, as in pscp secret_document.doc bjepson@www.as220.org:MyDocuments/.

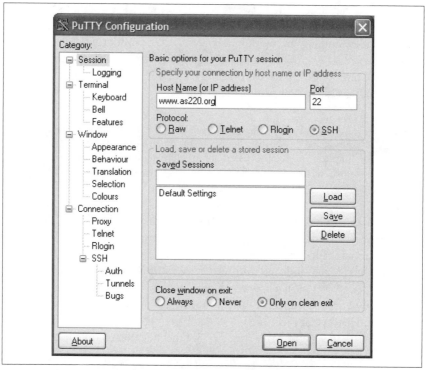

Figure 4-14. Connecting to a remote machine with PuTTY

Figure 4-15. PuTTY warns about unknown hosts

To use *psftp*, specify the hostname, and log in with your user ID and password. You can use ftp commands such as *put* (to upload a file to the server) and *get* (to download a file from the server):

```
C:\Documents and Settings\bjepson\My Documents>psftp www.as220.org
login as: bjepson
```

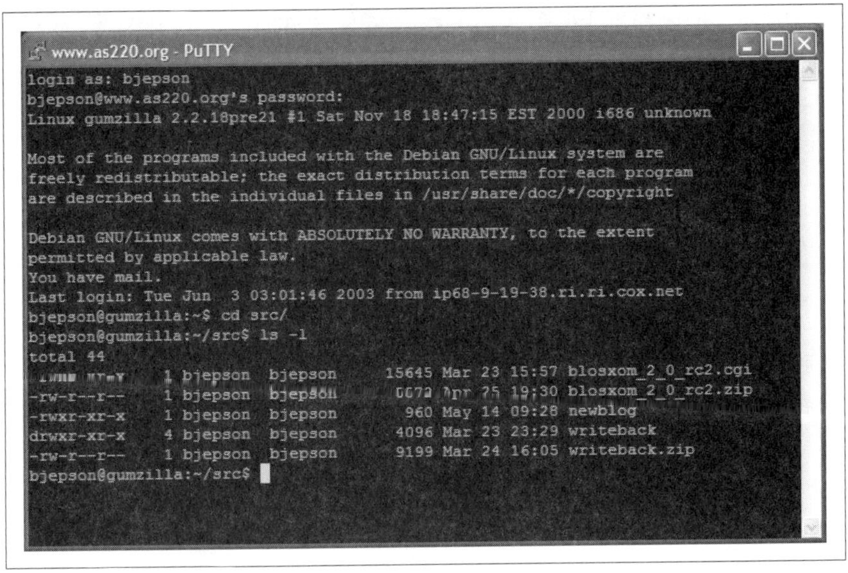

Figure 4-16. Using a Unix shell over a PuTTY connection

```
Using username "bjepson".
bjepson@www.as220.org's password:********
Remote working directory is /home/bjepson
psftp> cd MyDocuments
Remote directory is now /home/bjepson/MyDocuments
psftp> put secret_document.doc
local:secret_document.doc
       => remote:/home/bjepson/MyDocuments/secret_document.doc
psftp> get super_secret.doc
remote:/home/bjepson/MyDocuments/super_secret.doc
       => local:super_secret.doc
```

For more information, consult the PuTTY documentation and FAQ, located at the PuTTY home page.

Firewalls

A firewall keeps remote users from connecting to your computer, while letting you connect to remote servers. A Windows XP system includes a number of services, such as file sharing, that a remote attacker can use to access your system. In some cases, flaws in Windows can let a remote attacker gain complete control over your system (this is why it's important to run Windows Update frequently, so that you have the latest security updates).

Most wireless access points that have router capabilities also have built-in firewalls (and the firewall is typically enabled by default). But when you are on the road, you should enable Windows XP's firewall, because other users on the wireless network will be able to access your computer if you don't.

To enable the firewall for your wireless connection:

1. Open the Network Connections folder (Control Panel → Network and Internet Connections → Network Connections).

2. Right-click on your wireless connection and select Properties. When the connection Properties dialog appears, select the Advanced tab (Figure 4-17).

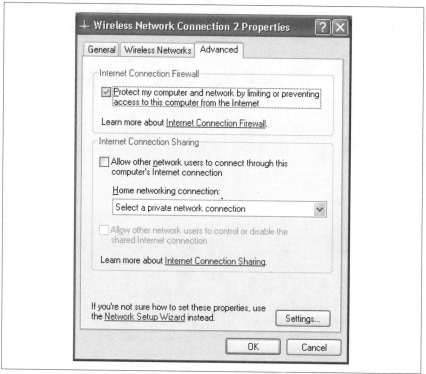

Figure 4-17. Enabling Windows XP's firewall

3. Check the box labeled "Protect my computer and network by limiting or preventing access to this computer from the Internet." This enables the basic firewall functionality.

4. Click Settings. This brings up the Advanced Settings dialog (Figure 4-18). Use the Services tab to configure the inbound services (such as Remote Desktop) that you want other users to have access to. Use the Security Logging tab to configure how connection attempts and failures are logged. The ICMP tab allows you to enable Internet Control Message Protocol (ICMP) requests, which are employed when remote users apply diagnostic utilities such as *ping* to verify whether your

computer is accessible. By leaving these disabled, you make it a little harder for attackers to find your computer or to determine potential vulnerabilities.

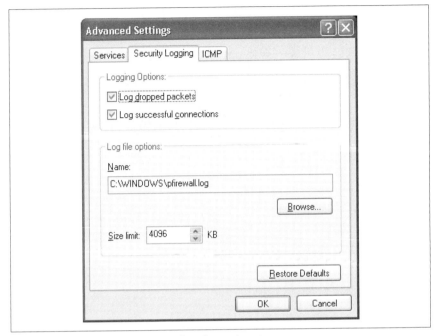

Figure 4-18. Configuring the firewall's advanced settings

5. Click OK to dismiss the Advanced Settings dialog, then click OK to dismiss the connection Properties dialog.

To see a log of connection attempts, open the file *C:\Windows\pfirewall.log* in a text editor.

Wi-Fi Security

Now that I have discussed the three ways to secure your wireless connection, I'll dive deep into the details of Wi-Fi security. A secure network should (ideally) have the following:

Authentication
   This is the process of verifying the identity of a user and making sure that she is who she claims. When you log in to your Windows computer, you are being authenticated via the username and password. In a Wi-Fi network, authentication comes into play when the access point has to determine whether a machine can connect to it.

Authorization

This is the process of allowing or denying access to a specific resource. You may be authenticated as a user, but you may not be authorized to use certain feature perhaps due to your user role (such as Guest, User, Power User, Administrator). For example, suppose you are at a wireless hotspot and have used up your allotted connection time: the network knows who you are, but won't authorize you to access the Internet until you pay for more minutes.

Confidentiality

This ensures the privacy of information that is being transmitted. Only an authorized party (such as the recipient of an email message) can see the information being transmitted. In a Wi-Fi network, confidentiality is supported by protocols such as WEP, WPA, and 802.1X, which encrypt the data that moves through the air.

Integrity

This ensures that the information that you have transmitted has not been tampered with en route to its destination.

Authentication, authorization, confidentiality, and integrity are also addressed by other systems on your network, just as they are on a wired network:

- Passwords can be used to authenticate users when they log into a file server.
- User roles control which files a given user has access to.
- Web and email communications can be secured with SSL.
- Network traffic can be tunneled through a VPN.

In Wi-Fi, there are two main authentication schemes (see Figure 4-19):

- Noncryptographic
- Cryptographic

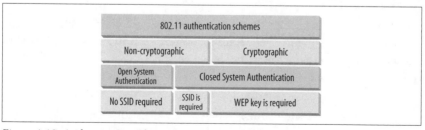

Figure 4-19. Authentication schemes

Under the noncryptographic scheme, you can authenticate in two ways: one without an SSID and one with an SSID. If a wireless network allows clients to connect to it without specifying an SSID, it is known as *Open System Authentication.*

For *Closed System Authentication,* two methods are possible: one using an SSID and one using a cryptographic key.

In an Open System Authentication scheme, there is no encryption performed on the packets transmitted between the client and the access point. The client does not need any SSID to join a network. This is the simplest mode as the configuration is straightforward and does not require any administration.

In the Closed System Authentication scheme, a client needs to specify an SSID that is identical to that specified by the access point in order to join the network. In addition, a shared key may also be used to encrypt the data packets transmitted between the client and the access point. In 802.11, the encryption method is known as Wired Equivalent Privacy (WEP), which we discuss in greater length in the section "Wired Equivalent Privacy (WEP)," next.

To get connected to a network in a closed system, a client must fulfill one or several of the following criteria:

1. The SSID of the client must match that of the access point. If a wireless access point has SSID broadcast turned on, your Windows XP computer should be able to detect its presence and allow you to connect to it. If the SSID broadcast is turned off, then the client must manually enter the SSID in order to associate with the access point. Getting associated with the access point is the first step in joining a network. Using an SSID to prevent people from accessing your network is not effective, since the SSID is often guessable and can be "sniffed" by network tools such as AiroPeek (more on this later).

 There are actually two steps to gaining network access. The first is *associating with the access point,* which means that the access point is willing to talk to your machine. The second step is *joining the network,* which usually means that your machine has been assigned an IP address and can talk to other hosts on the network. Unless I need to specifically discuss one or the other of these steps, I'll say "connected to the wireless network," which means that the client has been associated to the access point and joined the network.

2. Some access points use MAC address filtering to prevent clients from associating with them. You can enter a list of MAC addresses that you would allow (or deny) association with the access point (this is usually done through a web-based configuration interface on the access point). Even if a client has the correct SSID, if its MAC address is not listed in the allow-list of the access point, it cannot be associated with the access point. Again, using MAC address filtering to prevent unauthorized access to the network is not foolproof—an unauthorized user can easily change his network card's MAC address to that of an authorized client.

3. If WEP encryption is used on a wireless network, the client must specify the same WEP key as entered in the access point. Using a WEP key protects the data that is exchanged between the client and the access point. It also has the side effect of preventing unauthorized access to the network since a client needs the WEP key to encrypt and decrypt the packets exchanged. However, it has been proven that WEP is not secure and the WEP key can easily be recovered using freely available tools.

Wired Equivalent Privacy (WEP)

The main goal of WEP is to provide confidentiality of data packets. One secondary function of WEP is to provide authorization to a wireless network. This is, however, not the originally intended design goal of WEP (but see the section on 802.1X later in this chapter). Although WEP was initially designed to safeguard the confidentiality of the data in a wireless network, it has been proven to be insecure. To understand how WEP compromises your data in a wireless network, let's first understand how WEP works.

WEP uses the RC4 stream cipher algorithm (search the FAQ at *http://www.rsasecurity.com/rsalabs/faq* for "RC4"). It takes in a key and generates a larger pseudorandom bit sequence (the *key stream*) that serves as an encryption key. The key stream is then XOR'ed (a logical operation that returns true if one, but not both, of two binary values are true) with the original message (the *plaintext*) to produce the ciphertext.

When the recipient receives the encrypted stream (the *ciphertext*), it uses the shared key (to produce the same pseudorandom key stream) and performs an XOR function to derive the original message.

Here is how WEP uses RC4 to encrypt network communications:

1. Before encryption, the packet is run through an integrity check algorithm to generate a checksum. This is to prevent the message from being tampered with.

2. The 40-bit WEP key is then combined with the 24-bit Initialization Vector (IV) to form a 64-bit key.

3. RC4 then uses the 64-bit key to generate a keystream equal to the length of the plaintext to be encrypted (including the checksum generated by the integrity check algorithm in step 1).

4. The keystream is then XOR'ed with the plaintext to generate the encrypted packet. The IV is also appended in the header of the encrypted packet to create the ciphertext.

This encryption process is shown in Figure 4-20.

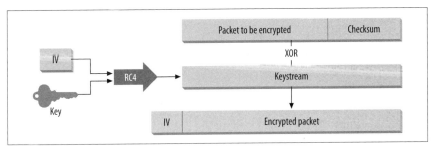

Figure 4-20. How WEP works

There are many security concerns that have been raised with respect to WEP. The first attack on WEP was identified by researchers Scott Fluhrer, Itsik Mantin, and Adi Shamir.

Here are some of the more important security concerns regarding WEP:

- The use of a shared static key is a major concern as everyone uses the same static key to secure his communications. As soon as the key is made known, the network is no longer secure. Some access points use a passphrase to generate keys, which makes it easier to guess the key, since people tend to use familiar terms for passphrases.

Distributing WEP keys in a large network is not feasible. Imagine trying to obtain a WEP key at the airport, or hassling a busy barista at Starbucks for one.

- The IV is only 24 bits in length, which means the same IV is reused many times over. This is especially true in a busy access point. Most network cards reset the IV to 0 when it is initialized, and increment the IV by 1 for each subsequent packet. (Although there are over 16 million different IVs, in practice you should begin to see the IVs repeat after more than 5000 packets are transmitted.) If an access point transmits packets of 1500 bytes in length, a 7 MB download would cause the same IV to be used again. It has been shown that when two eavesdroppers intercept two ciphertexts encrypted with the same keystream, it is possible to obtain the XOR of the two plaintexts. Over time, when more ciphertexts encrypted with the same keystream are collected, it is possible to recover the plaintext.

- If the keystream is recovered by an eavesdropper, forging a packet is easy, since you now have the keystream to generate the ciphertext. This can facilitate man-in-the-middle attacks, when a hacker may forge the identity of a legitimate user, and intercept and reroute the data transmitted.

- Due to the export regulations of the United States, the 802.11 standard called for 40-bit WEP only. Most vendors introduced longer key length for their products, making their products proprietary and often not interoperable. Even so, since WEP is not a well-designed cryptographic system, having extra key length does not make your communications more secure.

 Many vendors have claimed that their products support longer encryption keys such as 128 or 256 bits (which promises to be more secure). This is not technically correct. Because the 128-bit or 256-bit designation is inclusive of the 24-bit IV, the effective key lengths are 104 and 232 bits, respectively. However, some vendors do have products that support 152 bits (128 bit keys + 24-bit IV).

Figure 4-21 shows how you can enable WEP in a Linksys wireless router. For a 64-bit WEP key, only 40 bits (or 5 bytes) are specified by the user (since 24 bits are used by the IV). So for a 64-bit key, you need to enter 10 hexadecimal characters (since 2 hexadecimal characters make up 1 byte). For a 128-bit WEP key, 26 hexadecimal characters are needed.

Figure 4-21 also shows the Linksys wireless access point using a passphrase to generate four WEP keys. You can also manually set any of the four keys as your WEP key without using a passphrase. After you set the keys, click Apply.

 The wireless client enters one of the four keys specified in the Linksys access point and not the passphrase itself. The passphrase is used to simplify the task of generating the WEP key.

802.11i

A longer-term solution to resolve WEP's inadequacies lies in the hands of the IEEE workgroup TGi (*http://grouper.ieee.org/groups/802/11/Reports/tgi_update.htm*) when they complete the 802.11i specifications at the end of 2003.

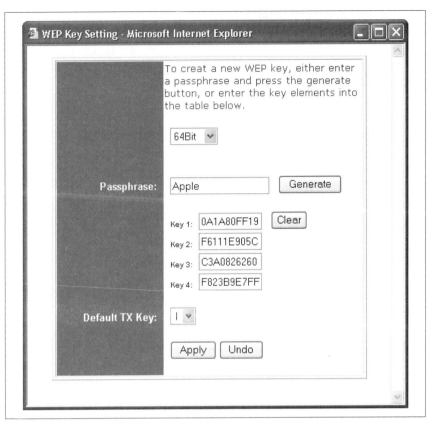

Figure 4-21. Setting WEP keys in the Linksys access point

Dynamic WEP Keys

Some vendors, like Cisco and 3COM, have implemented a dynamic WEP key in response to WEP's weaknesses. Per user session, Cisco's software generates a dynamic WEP key that is not shared with other users.

However, you must use access points, wireless cards, and adapters from the same vendor for dynamic WEP keys to work. For more information on Cisco's Dynamic WEP keys, visit *http://www.cisco.com/warp/public/cc/pd/ witc/ao350ap/prodlit/1281_pp.pdf.*

The 802.11i specifications will address the items in the list shown next.

Use of 802.1X for authentication

The 802.1X specification is a framework for mutual authentication between a client and the access point. It may also use a RADIUS-based authentication server and one of the Extensible Authentication Protocols (EAP) variations. 802.1X uses a new key for each session; hence it replaces WEP's static key.

Use of the Temporal Key Integrity Protocol (TKIP)

TKIP will be used as a short-term solution to WEP's flaws. It uses 128-bit dynamic keys that are utilized by different clients. Because of the changing keys, intruders would not have time to collect enough packets to compromise the security scheme.

Use of Advanced Encryption Standard (AES)

The full implementation of 802.11i will utilize the AES encryption system for enhanced encryption in access points. However, use of AES requires changes in the chipsets used in wireless devices; thus, at the time of this writing, no wireless device supports AES.

The 802.11i specification is tentatively called WPA2. See the next section for more details.

Wi-Fi Protected Access (WPA). While the industry is waiting for the 802.11i specification to be ratified, the Wi-Fi Alliance has addressed the present need for secure wireless communication by coming out with the Wi-Fi Protected Access (WPA).

 The WPA is also known as WPA1, while 802.11i is known as WPA2.

WPA is a subset of the 802.11i standard and will be forward compatible with it. The key components of WPA are:

802.1X

802.1X is a *port-based authentication mechanism*. See the next section for a detailed discussion of 802.1X.

TKIP technologies

TKIP provides data encryption enhancements including a per-packet key mixing function, a Message Integrity Check (MIC) called Michael, an extended Initialization Vector (IV) with sequencing rules, and a re-keying mechanism. In a nutshell, TKIP addresses WEP's limitations by having dynamic keys coupled with a much longer IV (which means that the chances of reusing the same IV within a period of time are reduced).

So how does WPA differ from WEP? Table 4-1 shows the quick comparison.

Table 4-1. Comparing WPA to WEP

	WPA	WEP
Key length	128-bit	40-bit to 232-bit
Key type	Dynamic key; per-user, per-session, per-packet keys	Static shared key; used by everyone in the network
Key distribution	Automatic key distribution	Each user must type in the key
Authentication	Uses 802.1X and EAP	Uses WEP key for authentication; flawed

WPA and Windows XP

Microsoft has recently released the WPA Wireless Security Update in Windows XP (*http://support.microsoft.com/?kbid=815485*).

The features of the security update are:

- 802.1X authentication
- WPA key management
- TKIP
- Michael
- AES support

However, before you start to use WPA, verify that your wireless card and access point both support it. Check with your vendor to see whether WPA can be supported via firmware upgrades.

802.1X Authentication

The 802.1X specification is a port-based network access control mechanism: when a client is authenticated, the port is granted access; if not, access to the port is denied. Although 802.1X was originally designed for Ethernet networks, it can be applied to wireless networks as well.

 In a wireless LAN, a port is simply the connection between a client and an access point.

This is how 802.1X works (see Figure 4-22):

1. The *Supplicant* (the client that wants to access a network resource) connects to the *Authenticator* (whose resource is needed).

2. The Authenticator asks for credentials from the Supplicant and passes the credentials to the *Authenticating Server*.

3. The Authenticating Server authenticates the Supplicant on behalf of the Authenticator.

4. If the Supplicant is authenticated, access is then granted.

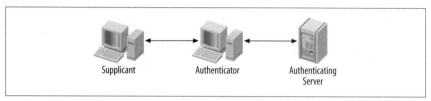

Figure 4-22. Authenticating a Supplicant in 802.1X

Note that before the authentication is performed, all the communications go through an *uncontrolled port*. After authentication, the *controlled port* is used.

For the Authentication Server to authenticate the Supplicant, the Point-to-Point Protocol Extensible Authentication Protocol (EAP) is used. EAP supports multiple authentication mechanisms and was originally developed for PPP.

In a wireless network, a wireless client needs to connect to an access point; in this case, the wireless access point is the Authenticator. The Authenticator can maintain a database of users and their respective passwords. However, this is a huge administrative task, especially in a large network. So an access point can be connected to a RADIUS (Remote Authentication Dial-In User Service) server, which will maintain the database of users and perform authentication on behalf of the access point. This is as shown in Figure 4-23.

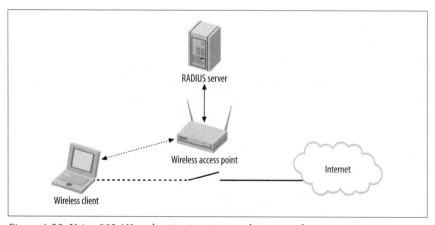

Figure 4-23. Using 802.1X authentication in a wireless network

Using a RADIUS server takes care of the authentication aspect of security only. What about confidentiality? Packets traveling between the wireless clients and the access point must be encrypted to ensure confidentiality.

When a client is validated at the RADIUS server, an authentication key is transmitted to the access point. (This key is encrypted; only the access point can decrypt it.) The access point then decrypts the key and uses it to create a new key specific to that wireless client. That key is sent to the wireless client, where it's used to encrypt the master global authentication key to the wireless client. To address WEP's shortcoming of a fixed key, the access point will generate a new master authentication key at regular intervals.

802.1X's Support in Access Points

At the time of this writing, support of 802.1X is mostly limited to enterprise-level access points. However, if you are lucky, your access point vendor may have firmware that allows your access point to be upgraded to support 802. 1X authentication. The D-Link 900AP+ supports 802.1X after a firmware upgrade. Best of all, it is a consumer access point that is affordable (under $100 in the U.S.).

Types of EAP. There are many variants of Extensible Authentication Protocol (EAP). Here are some that you may come across in wireless security literature:

EAP-MD5
   EAP-MD5 uses the challenge/response method to allow a server to authenticate a user using a username and password. MD5 does not provide mutual authentication and is vulnerable to an offline dictionary attack.

EAP-TLS (EAP-Transport Layer Security)
   EAP-TLS is based on X.509 (an ITU standard specifying the contents of a digital certificate) certificates. It is currently the most commonly used EAP type for securing wireless networks. However, EAP-TLS requires the use of PKI (Public Key Infrastructure), which is not feasible to be implemented on small networks.

PEAP (Protected EAP)
   To counter the complexity of using EAP-TLS, PEAP was proposed as an alternative. PEAP uses a server-side certificate to allow the authentication of the server. It creates an EAP-TLS tunnel and then uses other authentication methods over the tunnel. EAP methods such as MD5, MS-CHAP, and MS-CHAP v2 are supported. PEAP was proposed as an IETF standard by Microsoft, Cisco, and RSA.

EAP-TTLS (EAP Tunneled TLS)

EAP-TTLS is similar to PEAP. It creates a tunnel between the user and the RADIUS server. It supports EAP methods such as MD5, MS-CHAP, and MS-CHAP v2.

LEAP (Lightweight EAP)

LEAP is Cisco's proprietary version of EAP, which works mostly with Cisco's wireless cards, RADIUS servers, and access points.

MS-CHAP v2 (Microsoft Challenge-Handshake Authentication Protocol Version 2)

Originally designed by Microsoft as a PPP authentication protocol, MS-CHAP v2 is a password-based, challenge-response, mutual authentication protocol that uses the Message Digest 4 (MD4) and Data Encryption Standard (DES) algorithms to encrypt responses. MS-CHAP v2 is now an EAP type in Windows XP.

Windows XP (Service Pack 1) supports PEAP and EAP-TLS. Prior to Service Pack 1, EAP-TLS and EAP-MD5 are supported. Figure 4-24 shows the various layers of EAP and their relationships to 802.1X.

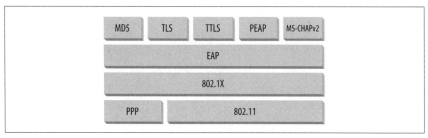

Figure 4-24. The variants of EAP and their relationships to 802.1X and 802.11

Using 802.1X in Windows XP

This section explains how to implement 802.1X authentication using PEAP and MS-CHAP v2 authentication methods in Windows XP. Using PEAP with MS-CHAP v2 authentication allows users to be authenticated using a username and password. This is much easier to administer than PEAP with EAP-TLS, which requires certificates to be installed on a user's computer. Also, PEAP with MS-CHAP v2 requires only a server certificate to be installed.

> If you are only interested in knowing how to log in to an 802.1X protected wireless network, you can skip to the section "Configuring the client," later in this chapter.

Configuring the RADIUS server (IAS). For this section, I assume you have the following:

- Windows 2000 Server SP3 or greater acting as a Domain controller using Active Directory.

- Microsoft 802.1X Authentication Client for Windows 2000 (*http://support.microsoft.com/default.aspx?scid=kb;en-us;313664*) installed on your computer. Although the word "client" appears in the name, this is a required component for the server.

> The Microsoft 802.1X Authentication Client for Windows 2000 contains support for PEAP, which is required if you specify the use of PEAP on the client side (this is supported in Windows XP if you install the "Windows XP Support Patch for Wireless Protected Access").
>
> Also, PEAP requires Certificate Services to be installed on your Windows 2000. You can install Certificate Services by going to the Control Panel and using Add/Remove Programs, then selecting Add/Remove Windows Components.

First, you must configure the RADIUS server (Internet Authentication Server) on the Windows 2000 Domain Controller:

1. Launch Internet Authentication Service (IAS) by clicking on Start → Programs → Administrative Tools → Internet Authentication Service (see Figure 4-25).

Figure 4-25. Registering IAS with Active Directory

2. Right-click on Internet Authentication Service (local) and select "Register Service in Active Directory".

3. Right-click on Clients and select "New Client".

4. Give a name to your client, say "AP" (which is your access point, the Authenticator).

5. Enter the IP address of the access point and check "Client must always send the signature attribute in the request". Enter a secret key to be known by both the access point and IAS.

6. Right-click on Remote Access Policies and select "New Remote Access Policy".

7. Give a name to your new policy, such as "Wireless access". Click Next.

8. Add an attribute. Select the "Day-And-Time-Restriction" attribute and click Add.

9. Choose the time that you want the user to be allowed access to the network. Select all available time slots, click Permitted, and click OK. Click Next.

10. Select the "Grant remote access permission" option to allow the remote user to log on if he is authenticated. Click Next.

11. Click on Edit Profile... to choose the authentication type.

12. Click the Authentication tab and select the options as shown in Figure 4-26. Click OK.

13. When prompted to read the help files on the EAP types checked, click No.

14. Click Finish to complete the setup.

Configuring Active Directory. Once the RADIUS server is configured, you need to give access permission to users in Active Directory.

1. Click on Start → Programs → Administrative Tools → Active Directory Users and Computers.

2. Click the Users item and double-click on the username that you want to grant wireless access to.

3. Select the Dial-in tab and select the Allow access option. Click OK.

Configuring the access point. Most consumer access points available today do not support 802.1X authentication. You would need to buy enterprise-level access points in order to use 802.1X authentication. Fortunately, a few consumer access points, such as the D-Link 900AP+, support 802.1X via a firmware download. If you own the D-Link 900AP+ access point, be sure to check out D-Link's web site to download the latest firmware. (If you purchased your access point after mid-2003, it may already have the firmware with 802.1X support).

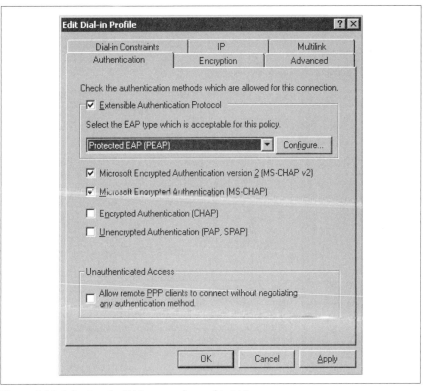

Figure 4-26. Selecting the EAP type to be used in IAS

You can administer the DWL-900AP+ access point using either a web-based utility or the provided Access Point Manager (see Figure 4-27). You can access the Access Point Manager by clicking Start → Programs → D-Link Airplus Access Point → D-Link AirPlus Manager.

To configure the DWL-900AP+ for 802.1X authentication, click on the 802.1X Setting link in the Access Point Manager (see Figure 4-27).

1. Turn on the 802.1X Function checkbox.

2. Select the length of the key and enter the information for the RADIUS server that you set up in the previous section.

 You need to enable WEP in order for 802.1X authentication to work.

3. The port number for the RADIUS server is 1812. You can specify up to two RADIUS servers. Also, enter the shared secret key that you entered in IAS.

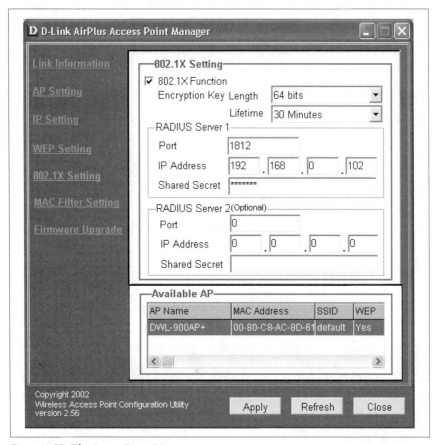

Figure 4-27. The Access Point Manager

Configuring the client. The last stage is configuring the client. This is also the stage for readers who are trying to log on to a network that uses 802.1X authentication.

 The test computer that I used for this book was updated with the Windows XP Support Patch for Wireless Protected Access (see *http://support.microsoft.com/?kbid=815485*). If you have not installed the patch, some of the screen elements may differ slightly.

1. Right-click on the Wireless Network Connection icon located in the Tray and select "View Available Wireless Networks" (see Figure 4-28).

2. Select the SSID of the network that you wish to connect to. In my case, *default* is the network that implements 802.1X authentication. Select default and enter the network (WEP) key for this network. Turn on the

Figure 4-28. Viewing the available wireless networks

checkbox "Enable IEEE 802.1X authentication for this network" (see Figure 4-29).

Figure 4-29. Selecting the default wireless network

3. Click on Advanced... to configure the settings for the selected network (see Figure 4-30).
4. Under the Available networks section, select default and click Configure.
5. Click the Authentication tab (see Figure 4-31).
6. For EAP type, select Protected EAP (PEAP) and click Properties.
7. Select Secured password (EAP-MSCHAP v2) as the authentication method (see Figure 4-32). Click Configure....

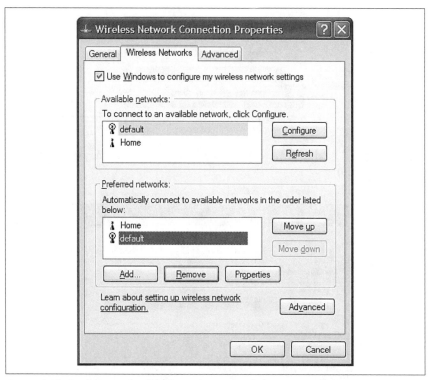

Figure 4-30. Configuring the default wireless network for 802.1X authentication

Fast Reconnect allows PEAP to quickly resume a TLS session. It minimizes the connection delay in wireless networks when a wireless device roams from one access point to another.

8. Turn off the checkbox "Automatically use my Windows logon name and password (and domain if any)" (see Figure 4-33). Click OK three times to complete the settings.

9. Finally, double-click the Wireless Network Connection icon located in the Tray again and connect to the *default* network. You will be asked to supply your credentials to log on to the network (see Figure 4-34).

10. Enter your username and password; if you are a valid user (see Figure 4-35), you will be connected to the network.

To confirm that you are connected to the network, launch your web browser and see if you can connect to the Internet. You may also use the ipconfig /all command to see whether you are assigned an IP address.

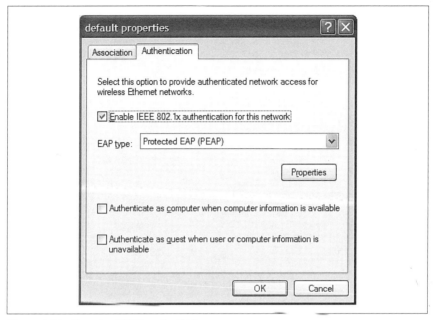

Figure 4-31. Choosing PEAP as the EAP type

Are 802.11 Networks Really Secure?

One of the problems with wireless security is that you don't need expensive tools to break into a wireless network. All you need in your toolbox is a computer, a wireless card, some suitable software, and perhaps a good antenna for receiving wireless signals.

The following is a list of software that you can use to detect wireless networks, sniff wireless packets in transit, and much more. These tools have numerous legitimate uses, such as detecting unauthorized access points, intrusion detection, network traffic analysis, and debugging networked applications such as a web server.

NetStumbler (http://www.netstumbler.com/)
> NetStumbler is a free application that allows you to detect the presence of wireless networks. Using NetStumbler, you can obtain information about a particular access point, the SSID used, whether WEP is enabled, and so on. Coupled with a GPS, you can even pinpoint the location of an access point. NetStumbler is often used for Wardriving, site surveys, and detecting rogue access points.

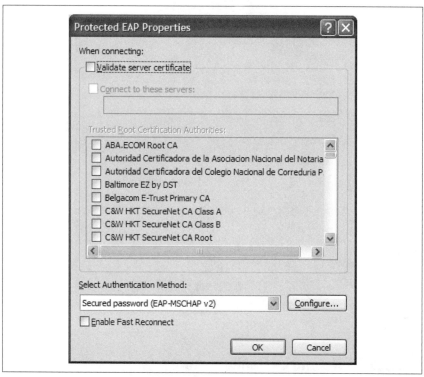

Figure 4-32. Choosing the authentication method

Figure 4-33. Disabling automatic Windows logon

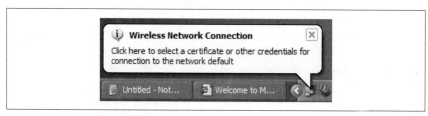

Figure 4-34. Prompting for the user credentials

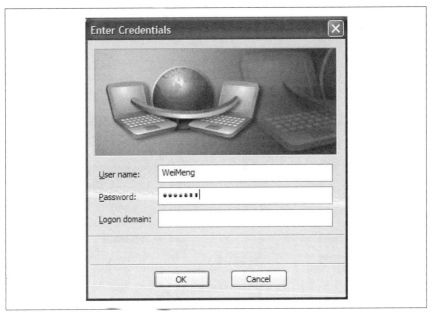

Figure 4-35. Logging in to the RADIUS server

AiroPeek NX (http://www.airopeek.com/)

AiroPeek is a wireless LAN analyzer from WildPackets. It is an extremely powerful wireless LAN analyzer that most security professionals use (be forewarned, this package costs $3499!). AiroPeek is able to sniff raw wireless packets transmitted through the air, which is why protecting your wireless network with 802.1X, a VPN, SSH, or even WEP is important. Data packets that are not encrypted can easily be sniffed by AiroPeek.

Ethereal (http://www.ethereal.com/)

Ethereal is a free network protocol analyzer for Unix and Windows computers. It is similar to AiroPeek in that it allows you to sniff wireless (and wired) packets in transit. Many network protocols are susceptible to sniffing in this manner. For example, Telnet and FTP both send passwords as plaintext (for secure alternatives, see the section "Secure Shell (SSH)," earlier in this chapter). Figure 4-36 shows an Ethereal session capturing an FTP password.

AirSnort (http://airsnort.shmoo.com/)

AirSnort is a wireless LAN analyzer with the capability of recovering WEP keys. It does so by passively collecting packets that have been transmitted. After collecting enough packets, AirSnort is able to recover the WEP key.

All this software works in Windows XP, except for AirSnort, which runs on Linux. A Windows version is in the works, but for now, only Linux is supported.

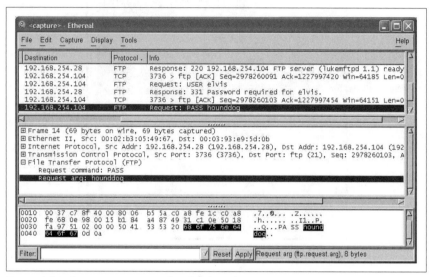

Figure 4-36. Capturing a password with Ethereal

Common Security Features on Access Points

Most wireless access points provide some degree of protection against unauthorized access to the network. Here are a few common features found in most consumer access points:

Disabling SSID broadcast

Disabling SSID broadcast causes the access point to suppress the broadcast of SSID information to wireless clients. In order to join the wireless network, a wireless client needs to manually specify the SSID that the network uses, or else it will not be able to associate with the access point.

MAC address filtering

Most access points support MAC address filtering by allowing only network cards with the specified MAC addresses to be associated with them. In a small network, this is feasible but it becomes administratively prohibitive in a large network. Note that MAC address filtering authenticates a device, not a user.

IP filtering

IP filtering works just like MAC address filtering, but instead filters computers based on IP addresses.

Network Address Translation (NAT)

NAT allows multiple computers to connect to the Internet by sharing a single public IP address. One side effect of this is that computers within the internal network are shielded against the outside parties, since the IP addresses used are only valid within the network.

802.1X

As 802.1X gains acceptance, expect to see support of 802.1X in consumer access points, not just enterprise-level access points. Check with your vendor to see if your access point supports 802.1X authentication (or can be upgraded to do so via a firmware upgrade).

In the following sections, I discuss some of the common techniques used for securing wireless networks, and their effectiveness.

MAC address filtering. While MAC address filtering can prevent unauthorized network devices from gaining entry to a network, there are two problems with it:

- It is the device that is authenticated in MAC address filtering, not the user. Hence if a user loses the network card, another user who picks up the network card is able to gain access to the network without any problem.

- MAC addresses can easily be spoofed. Using AiroPeek, it is easy to impersonate the MAC address of another device. Also, if you are a little adventurous, you can try changing the MAC address of your wireless card manually in Windows XP. Visit *http://www.klcconsulting.net/ Change_MAC_w2k.htm* for more information.

Disabling SSID broadcast. Disabling SSID broadcast prevents uninvited users from accessing the network. However, there are two fundamental flaws with this approach:

- It is not difficult to guess the SSID of a network. Most users deploy wireless networks using the default SSID that comes with the access point. It is too easy to guess the SSID of a wireless network based on hints like the brand of the access point, or from clues like the thrown-away box of the access point.

- When you disable SSID broadcast, the access point does not broadcast the SSID information. However, as soon as one user connects to the access point using the known SSID, it is possible to sniff the SSID that is transmitted in the network. Hence this method is only secure if there is no user on the network; but as soon as one user is on the network, the SSID is no longer a secret.

Using WEP. As we have discussed, WEP has some fundamental flaws that make it prone to hackers. For example, AirSnort can recover the WEP key after collecting a sizeable number of packets from the wireless network.

Transferring in plaintext. Even though WEP is not secure, it is still advisable to use it to at least make it somewhat difficult to breach your network. Site surveys will often show that the majority of wireless networks do not use WEP! Using AiroPeek or Ethereal, it is very easy to examine the data transmitted across the air.

CHAPTER FIVE

Configuring Wireless Access Points

So far you have been learning about how wireless networks work and how to connect to one. In this chapter, I show you how to deploy a wireless network yourself. I illustrate this using two different wireless access points and considering how they might be used in two different environments—one at home and another in the office. Of course, many home users will have needs that are closer to that of an office, and some small offices may have needs closer to that of a home user. For the purposes of these examples, the home environment is assumed to have consumer-level broadband access, while the office environment is assumed to have a more extensive wired network in place.

Setting Up a Wireless Network

The cost for setting up a wireless network has, over the years, been lowered substantially. Today, you can easily set up a wireless network at home for about $200. For that amount, you can get a wireless access point, a wireless PC card (for your notebook), and a USB wireless adapter (for your desktop).

 In this section, I am assuming you want your wireless users to access the Internet. If your aim is to simply connect two machines wirelessly, you do not need a DSL/ADSL modem and wireless access point. All you need is a wireless adapter or card for each computer. See the section on "Ad-Hoc Wireless Networking" later in this chapter.

To set up your own wireless network, you need the following:

- A DSL/ADSL or cable modem with an Ethernet connector (you may also have satellite Internet or a T1 line)
- A wireless access point with router functionality

- A wireless access card or adapter for each machine that wants to get on the wireless network

 Some ISPs, in an attempt to discourage multiple computers from sharing the Internet connection, will bundle a USB-port modem when you sign up for the broadband package. In order to connect a router to your ISP, you'll need to purchase a separate modem with an Ethernet port that is compatible with your ISP. Check with your ISP to obtain a list of compatible modems.

A typical wireless home/office setup is shown in Figure 5-1 (note that the PC with Ethernet connection is optional).

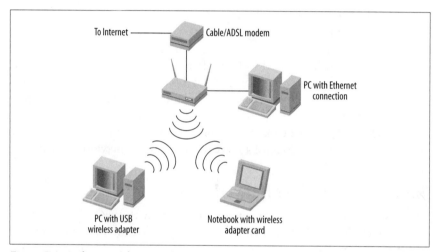

Figure 5-1. Architecture for a wireless network

Wireless Access Points

A wireless access point is a wireless device that routes traffic in a wireless network. It is usually attached to an existing wired network, or to a Wide Area Network (WAN) connection such as a cable or DSL/ADSL modem. Basically, the purpose of the wireless access point is to provide a centralized location for exchanging wireless traffic sent by wireless devices. Wireless access points generally come in two flavors:

- Pure wireless access point
- Wireless access point with router functionality

Pure wireless access points. A pure wireless access point simply comes with an Ethernet connector for connecting to a wired network. This is suitable for situations where you already have an established network and simply want to enable wireless access to it. It relies on your network to provide DHCP (Dynamic Host Configuration Protocol—a protocol that assigns IP addresses to clients) services, and hence is not suitable in environments in which a single IP address is usually allocated, such as in a home network. A pure wireless access point is little more than a virtual wire that connects your unwired computers to whatever networking hardware you've plugged the access point into.

Figure 5-2 shows the Linksys WAP11 Wireless Access Point.

Figure 5-2. The Linksys WAP11 Wireless Access Point (802.11b) (photo courtesy of Linksys)

 If you're connecting an access point to an ISP, you should check with your ISP to see if it will allocate more than one IP address. If only one IP address is allocated, you will need a router with DHCP services to allow multiple computers to connect to the Internet. In such a configuration, your router will grab that one IP address and use Network Address Translation (NAT) to share that address with the rest of your network (see the sidebar "DHCP and NAT," later in this chapter). Even if your ISP offers more than one IP address, you should go with a wireless access point that has firewall capabilities, which nearly always go hand-in-hand with router capabilities. You will only pay a little bit more for a router, but the peace of mind that comes with a firewall is well worth it.

Figure 5-3 shows the back of the Linksys WAP11.

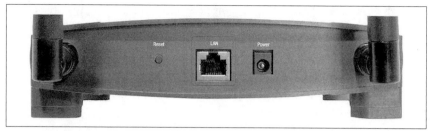

Figure 5-3. The back of a wireless access point (photo courtesy of Linksys)

At the moment, there are three prevailing wireless standards: 802.11b, 802.11a, and 802.11g (see Chapter 2). Figure 5-4 shows the D-Link DWL-6000AP Multimode Wireless Access Point that supports both the 802.11a and 802.11b wireless standards.

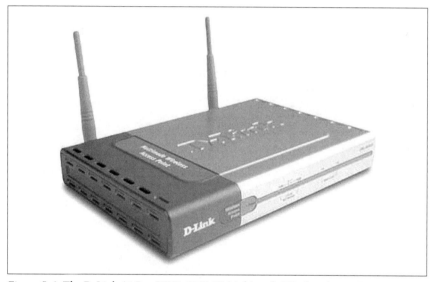

Figure 5-4. The D-Link AirPro DWL-6000AP Multimode Wireless Access Point (802.11a and 802.11b)

Besides the 802.11a wireless access points, vendors are also launching new 802.11g wireless access points based on the 802.11g specifications. Figure 5-5 shows the Linksys WAP54G Wireless Access Point that supports both the 802.11b and 802.11g wireless standards.

Wireless access points with router. A wireless access point with router functionality, on the other hand, provides routing services in addition to being a wireless access point. It comes with a port for connecting to the WAN, and it also usually comes with a multiport switch for wired connections (see

Figure 5-5. The Linksys WAP54G Wireless Access Point (802.11b and 802.11g) (photo courtesy of Linksys)

Figure 5-6). Most routers support DHCP and come with NAT services (see the "DHCP and NAT" sidebar later in this chapter for more information). As such, a wireless access point with router functionality is useful in situations in which only a single IP address is allocated, or in which a router's firewall services are needed. Most DSL/ADSL and cable connections are allocated a single IP address, effectively enabling only a single machine to connect at any one time. With a wireless router, multiple computers can connect to the Internet simultaneously.

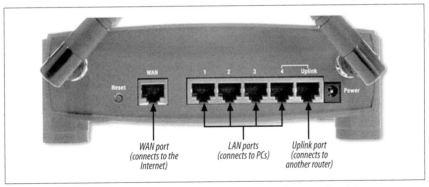

Figure 5-6. The back of a wireless access point with router functionality (photo courtesy of Linksys)

Figure 5-7 shows the Linksys BEFW11SE Wireless Access Point with a 4-port switch.

Figure 5-7. The Linksys BEFW11SE Wireless Access Point with 4-port switch (802.11b) (photo courtesy of Linksys)

For 802.11g, D-Link has the DI-624, as shown in Figure 5-8.

Figure 5-8. The D-Link DI-624 AirPlus Extreme G Wireless Access Point with Router (802.11b and 802.11g)

Setting up multiple access points. If you have a traditional wired network in your office or home environment, you can enable wireless access by installing a wireless access point in your network. For a physically large access area, you can use multiple access points. Figure 5-9 shows three wireless access points connected to a wired network.

These wireless access points might all be configured with the same Service Set Identifier (SSID) or with different SSIDs. If their ranges overlap with one

DHCP and NAT

DHCP (Dynamic Host Configuration Protocol) automatically assigns an IP address to computers when they are logged on to the network. With DHCP, each machine is given an IP address (with an expiration date and time) during the time that they are on the network. When they are logged off the network, the IP address is reused and reassigned to another computer.

Most home networks (DSL/ADSL or cable access) are usually given a single IP address, which means that only one machine is able to connect to the Internet at any one time. However, multiple machines can connect to the Internet using NAT (Network Address Translation). Most routers support NAT; the router is assigned that single IP address, and computers connected to the router are assigned IP addresses that are only valid within the local network (and are unusable on the Internet at large). For packets that are sent out into the Internet, the router translates these local IP addresses into the real IP address that the router holds. The reverse happens when a packet from the Internet is sent to a machine on the local network. The NAT looks into its address translation table and maps it into the local IP address used by the computer on the local network.

In summary, DHCP allocates dynamic IP addresses to computers connected to the router while NAT allows all these computers with different IP addresses to communicate with the external network via a single IP address.

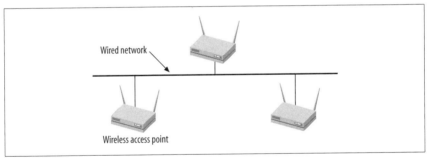

Figure 5-9. Adding wireless access points to your wired network

another's, you may get a more reliable signal by assigning each one to a different channel (see "Channels" in Chapter 2 and "Determining wireless coverage with NetStumbler" in Chapter 3).

If users need to roam from one access point to another, it is recommended that all the access points be configured with the same SSID. If not, the user may not be able to move from one access point to another unless they configure their computers to accept different SSIDs. The sidebar "Windows XP Wireless Zero Configuration" in Chapter 2 explains how to configure your computer to accept different SSIDs.

In general, Windows XP automatically detects the SSIDs of the wireless networks, unless the access point turns off SSID broadcast. Please refer to Chapter 4 for more information on turning off SSID broadcast.

The Vivato Switch

Instead of using multiple access points to wirelessly enable your office, you could just plug in a Vivato indoor wireless switch to your existing network. The Vivato switch is a flat-panel wireless switch that mounts on a wall. It contains a collection of antennas that shoot narrow, focused beams at wireless clients. Unlike other access points, Vivato claims to be able to give each wireless client maximum throughput, and a single Vivato switch can cover the entire office floor, penetrating glass buildings and obstacles. But all these neat features come with a hefty price tag: U.S. $8995.

Visit *http://www.vivato.net/* for more information.

Using the wireless access point as a repeater. Every wireless access point has a limited operating range. To extend the effective range of a wireless network, you can use a wireless repeater. There aren't many standalone wireless repeaters in the market, but some wireless access points double as a repeater. Figure 5-10 show how a wireless repeater can extend the effective range of a wireless network.

You need to use compatible wireless access points with the repeater you are using. In other words, you would most likely buy the equipment from the same vendors.

A wireless repeater does not need to connect to any part of the wired network. Basically it receives a signal from a wireless access point and retransmits it, essentially extending the range of the wireless network.

The D-Link AirPlus DWL-900AP+ Wireless Access Point is one such access point that includes a repeating function (see Figure 5-11).

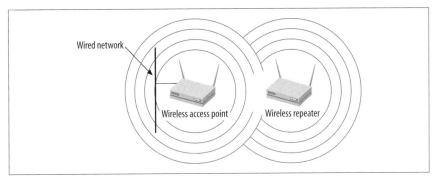

Figure 5-10. Using a wireless repeater to extend the range of a wireless network

Figure 5-11. The D-Link AirPlus DWL-900AP+ Wireless Access Point with repeating function

Using the wireless access point as a bridge. Another use of wireless access points is to bridge devices to connect two wired networks. Figure 5-12 shows this scenario.

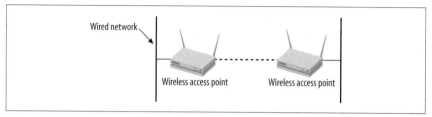

Figure 5-12. Using access points as wireless bridging devices

Two wired networks may be physically separated but can be linked using two wireless access points operating in bridge mode. The D-Link DWL-900AP+ supports this bridge mode.

Case Study: The Home Network

Figure 5-13 shows the Motorola SB4200 cable modem popularly used to connect to residential broadband services. Many users have ADSL/DSL modems instead of cable; some users even have satellite Internet access. Regardless of whether you use cable, ADSL/DSL, or satellite, you should have a device (such as the cable modem shown in Figure 5-13) with flashing lights and an Ethernet port that provides you with Internet access. You may have bought this device in a computer store or directly from your ISP, or perhaps you rent it from your ISP.

 Some ISPs may have supplied you with a device that uses a USB connection to your computer instead of Ethernet, or even a card that was installed inside your computer. To connect your broadband service to a wireless network, you'll need an external device with an Ethernet port. You may need to contact your ISP's technical support, explain what you are trying to do (give them the simplest version of the story: you're trying to connect a wireless access point to your broadband service), and request the correct device. If your ISP refuses to help or doesn't understand your request, it is time to find a new ISP.

A common limit of broadband connections is that only one computer can be connected to the Internet at any one time. As discussed in Chapter 2, there are many ways the ISP can impose the restriction, such as MAC address locking, or issuing a single IP address to the cable modem. So to enable multiple computers to wirelessly access the Internet, you could use a wireless

Figure 5-13. The Motorola SB4200 cable modem

router. (See the sidebar "DHCP and NAT" earlier in this chapter for information on how DHCP and NAT features found in wireless routers work around this limitation.) One such wireless router is the Linksys BEFW11S4 802.11b Wireless Access Point with 4-port switch (see Figure 5-14).

Figure 5-14. The Linksys BEFW11SE Wireless Access Point with 4-port switch (802.11b)

In most cases, this limit is a practical limitation dictated by the scarcity of IP addresses. Most ISPs permit you to use a router to get around this restriction, and some will happily sell you a router and may also send a technician to your home to set it up (often for an extra fee, but this is sometimes included with the purchase of a router). However, in some cases, your ISP's Terms of Service (TOS) may contractually limit you to one computer, in which case they will typically charge you a nominal fee for each additional computer to which you connect. If so, then using a router is a violation of the TOS. This was more common during the early days of broadband; nowadays, most ISPs don't care how many computers you connect, as long as they are your computers and you aren't sharing your connection with the rest of your neighborhood.

Figure 5-15 shows one possible configuration for a home network.

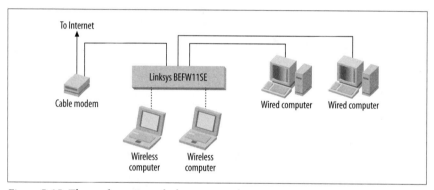

Figure 5-15. The configuration of a home network

See "Configuring an Access Point," later in this chapter, for information on setting up and configuring the BEFW11S4.

Case Study: The Office Network

Your office might have a router that allows your computers to access the network and Internet. You would most likely be using DHCP to obtain IP addresses for all the computers. (If your office doesn't have any of this, perhaps you are starting from scratch—in that case, your office will resemble a home network in that your wireless access point is your first foray into networking.) In this section, I discuss the issues involved with adding a wireless network to an office environment using the D-Link DI-714P+ Wireless Access Point as an example.

Rogue Access Points

Be sure to check with your administrator before you connect your access point to your network switch. End users who deploy wireless networks without the permission of the administrator pose a security risk, since wireless networks are generally not adequately protected. These unauthorized access points are known as rogue access points.

Also, do not connect an access point to a hub; connect it to a switch instead. Hubs are broadcast devices, and so all the packets received by a port in a hub will be broadcast to the wireless segment if an access point is connected to a hub.

The D-Link DI-714P+ (see Figure 5-16) is an enhanced 802.11b wireless access point with router functionality. It comes with AirPlus technology that allows up to 22 Mbps of data transfer rate if used together with D-Link's AirPlus wireless card (such as the D-Link DWL-650+). Besides this, it also includes a printer port for connecting a printer, so the access point can also act as a print server.

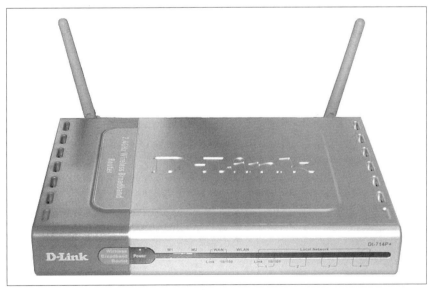

Figure 5-16. The D-Link DI-714P+ Wireless Router

Figure 5-17 shows the network configuration.

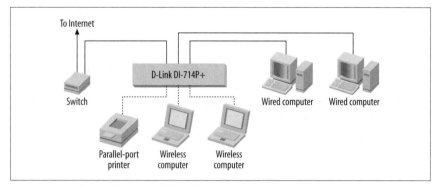

Figure 5-17. The configuration of an office network

As shown in Figure 5-17, the DI-714P+'s WAN port is plugged into the switch. Your desktop systems can be connected either to the switch or the LAN ports of the DI-714P+ (see Figure 5-18).

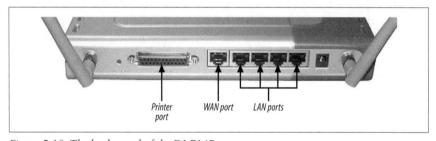

Printer   WAN port   LAN ports
port

Figure 5-18. The back panel of the DI-714P+

Configuring an Access Point

To connect your access point to the Internet, use a straight-through Ethernet cable to plug the access point's WAN port into your cable modem, DSL modem, router, or whatever piece of equipment in your home or office that is responsible for providing Internet access. After you plug it in, turn on the access point's switch (assuming it has one—some access points can only be powered down by unplugging them), and it will power up, perform its initialization, and then request a DHCP address from the cable or DSL modem or router.

You may need to reboot your cable or ADSL/DSL modem in order for the access point to obtain an IP address. This is especially important in cases where the modem was initially connected directly to the PC and may have locked itself to the MAC address of the PC (see the sidebar "Locking MAC Addresses" in Chapter 2).

Web-Based Configuration

To configure the wireless router, connect your computer to one of the wireless router's LAN ports using a straight-through Ethernet cable (if your computer has an autosensing Ethernet port, you can use either a straight-through or crossover cable). For the Linksys BEFW11S4, load the following URL in your web browser: *http://192.168.1.1/*. For the D-Link DI-714P+, use *http://192.168.0.1/*. When prompted for a username and password, use "admin" as your username and leave the password field empty.

 The default IP address, username, and password may be different for different access point models and manufacturers. Check your access point manual for the correct defaults.

Bypassing a Proxy Server

If you use a proxy server to connect to the Web, ensure that you bypass the router's IP address or you may not be able to connect to the web-based configuration utility.

To do so, go to Internet Explorer and follow these steps:

1. Click on Tools → Internet Options...
2. Select the Connection tab and click on LAN settings...
3. Check the option "Bypass proxy server for local addresses"

Figure 5-19 shows the web-based configuration utility of the BEFW11S4.

Figure 5-20 shows the web-based configuration utility of the DI-714P+. There are several tabs displayed horizontally: Home, Advanced, Tools, Status, and Help. Corresponding to each tab are various functions displayed vertically. For example, in the Home tab there are five functions: Wizard, Wireless, WAN, LAN, and DHCP.

DI-714P+ setup wizard. To quickly set up the DI-714P+, I suggest you run the wizard. Click on the Run Wizard button and take the following steps:

1. Change the password of the DI-714P+ (see Figure 5-21). Failing to change the default empty password will allow unauthorized users to access the router and make modifications that compromise the security of the network.
2. Choose the time zone settings for your router.

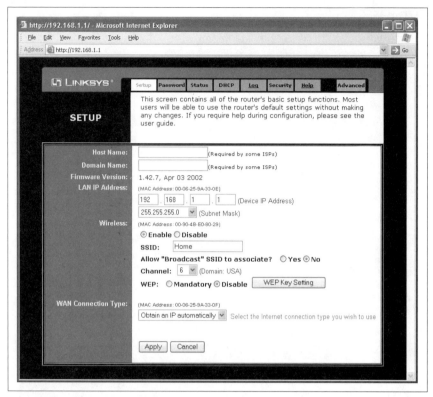

Figure 5-19. The BEFW11S4 configuration utility

3. Select the Internet connection type (see Figure 5-22). Choose Dynamic IP Address if your wired network supports DHCP. In a case where you are allocated a fixed IP address, choose Static IP Address. Most ADSL/DSL users will choose "PPP over Ethernet".

4. Depending on the connection type you have selected in Step 3, you will be asked to enter information pertaining to the selected connection type. Figure 5-23 shows the window displayed if you select Dynamic IP Address in Step 3. You can clone your network card's MAC address here.

 Please refer to Chapter 2 for an explanation of MAC address cloning.

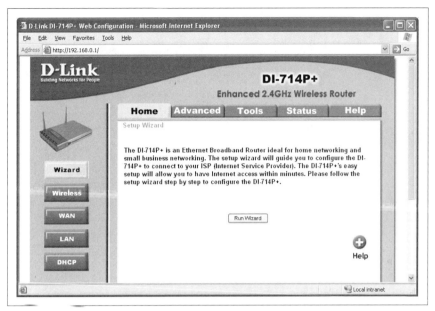

Figure 5-20. The configuration utility of the DI-714P+

Figure 5-21. Changing the password of the DI-714P+

5. Enter an SSID for your network. You can also set a channel to use here (see Figure 5-24). If you have multiple access points in a network, set them to use nonoverlapping channels (see Chapter 2 for more information on nonoverlapping channels). For WEP encryption, you have three choices: 64 bits, 128 bits, or 256 bits. Depending on the strength of the encryption, you would need to enter 10, 26, or 58 hexadecimal (0 to 9, A to F, or a to f) characters.

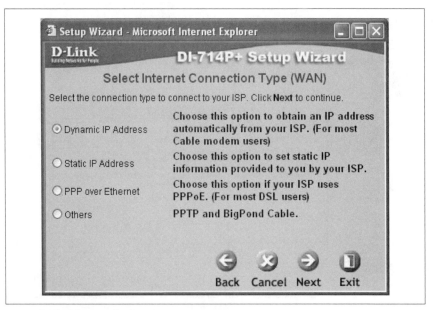

Figure 5-22. Selecting the Internet connection type

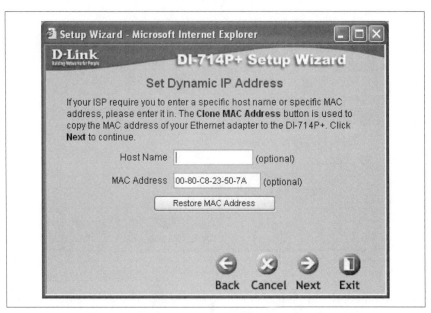

Figure 5-23. Setting the MAC address of the DI-714P+

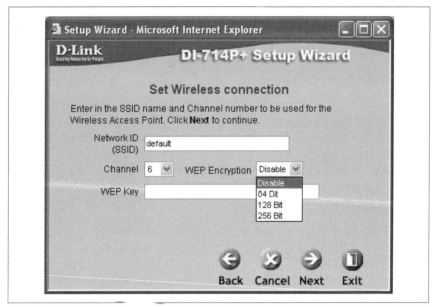

Figure 5-24. Using WEP encryption

  Chapter 4 discusses WEP keys in more detail.

That's it! Restart (switch off and switch on the router) the DI-714P+ for the new settings to take effect. Now, use an Ethernet cable and connect the WAN port of the DI-714P+ to the switch (or directly to the customer premise equipment supplied by your ISP, in case the DI-714P+ is the only switch you plan to use). You should now be able to use your computer with a wireless card (see Chapter 2) to connect to the Internet through the DI-714P+.

The configuration screen for different access point models, as well as access points from other manufacturers, will vary somewhat. The remaining sections explain how to accomplish common tasks with the web-based configuration.

Setting the SSID

The SSID (Service Set Identifier) gives your access point a name (see the section "SSID" in Chapter 2). If you intend to let strangers connect to your access point, I suggest you give your SSID a friendly name such as "welcome." (If you don't, be sure to see the sections "Enabling WEP" and "MAC Address Filtering" in this chapter).

To change the SSID of the BEFW11S4, click on the Setup tab, enter the new SSID, and select the appropriate channel number. To change the SSID of the DI-714P+, click on the Home tab and select the Wireless option.

Setting the Channel Number

If you have multiple access points in close proximity to one another, you should set them to broadcast on different channels. To change the channel number of the BEFW11S4, click on the Setup tab, enter the new SSID, and select the appropriate channel number. To change the SSID of the DI-714P+, click on the Home tab and select the Wireless option.

Enabling WEP

You can also enable WEP encryption to secure your wireless network. If you use WEP, users will not be able to connect to your network unless they know (or can obtain) the WEP key. Chapter 4 goes into more detail about using WEP (and stronger systems) to secure your wireless network.

To enable WEP on the BEFW11S4 (64- and 128-bit keys are supported), click on the WEP Key Setting button. You can specify up to four keys for WEP. You can also enter a passphrase to get the router to generate the four keys required. To enable WEP on the DI-714P+ (64-, 128-, and 256-bit WEP keys are supported), click the Home tab and select the Wireless option. As with the BEFW11S4, you can specify up to four keys.

The DI-714P+ does not support generating WEP keys using a passphrase.

Changing the Access Point's Default IP Address

By default, when a wireless client connects to the access point, it is assigned an IP address by the access point. The default LAN IP address for the BEFW11S4 itself is 192.168.1.1. The default IP address for the DI-714P+ is 192.168.0.1.

A wireless router has two IP addresses—one for LAN (Local Area Network) access and one for WAN (Wide Area Network) access. The LAN IP address (for example, 192.168.1.1) is used internally within your home or office wireless network. The WAN address (for example, 202.156.1.35) is for communicating with the outside world (in this case, assigned by your ISP).

You can modify the default LAN IP address of the BEFW11S4 by clicking the Setup tab and selecting the LAN IP Address option. You can modify the default IP address of the DI-714P+ by clicking on the Home tab and selecting the LAN option.

When the default IP address is changed, the range of allocatable IP addresses also changes. To learn how to change the range, see the later section "Configuring DHCP."

Be sure to enable the DHCP server on the wireless router if your ISP allocates only a single IP address to you. This allows multiple wireless users to connect to the Internet.

Setting the WAN IP Address

The BEFW11S4 supports five ways to obtain a WAN IP address:

Obtain an IP address automatically
Under this configuration, your ISP assigns you a different IP address periodically using DHCP

Static IP
With this configuration, your ISP gives you a static IP address. This is often found with commercial and hobbyist accounts where there's a need to run servers (such as a web or gaming server).

PPPoE (PPP over Ethernet)
This is a protocol used by many ADSL providers to encapsulate the Point-to-Point Protocol (PPP) within Ethernet. Among other things, it allows multiple users to be serviced through a single DSL modem.

RAS (Remote Access Service)
This is a protocol used by Windows for remote access. SingTel, a large ISP in Singapore, uses this.

PPTP (Point-to-Point Tunneling Protocol)
This is a protocol used for Virtual Private Networks (VPN), and is commonly used to establish a secure connection to a corporate network.

If your ISP allocates an IP address to you automatically, choose "Obtain an IP address automatically". If you use a static IP address, choose "Static IP". For most ADSL/DSL modem users, choose "PPPoE".

The DI-714P+ also supports Dynamic IP Address, Static IP Address, PPPoE, and PPTP.

Forgotten the IP Address of Your Wireless Router?

Suppose you have changed the LAN IP address of your wireless router and a month later you need to configure the router again. But, what is the IP address of the router? If you've forgotten, there are two ways to solve this problem:

1. Most wireless routers come with a reset button to restore the router back to its default factory settings. Doing so resets the router back to its original default IP address (which you can look up in the manual). But doing so also erases all the other settings. This is especially painful if you have entered the MAC addresses of all the network cards used for MAC address filtering. Note that some routers do have a backup utility to allow you to back up your settings.

2. Use the `ipconfig /all` command to see the default gateway IP address (wireless router). You will see something like the following. The Default Gateway is then your wireless router.

```
Ethernet adapter Wireless Network Connection:

        Connection-specific DNS Suffix  . :
        Description . . . . . . . . . . . :
          Cisco Systems 350 Series Wireless LAN Adapter
        Physical Address. . . . . . . . . :
          00-40-96-40-7E-F9
        Dhcp Enabled. . . . . . . . . . . : Yes
        Autoconfiguration Enabled . . . . : Yes
        IP Address. . . . . . . . . . . . : 192.168.2.101
        Subnet Mask . . . . . . . . . . . : 255.255.255.0
        Default Gateway . . . . . . . . . : 192.168.2.1
        DHCP Server . . . . . . . . . . . : 192.168.2.1
        DNS Servers . . . . . . . . . . . : 202.156.1.58
                                            202.156.1.48
        Lease Obtained. . . . . . . . . . :
          Tuesday, May 06, 2003 7:23:33 PM
        Lease Expires . . . . . . . . . . :
          Wednesday, May 07, 2003 7:23:33 PM
```

But what if you have forgotten your *password* to the router? Well, then the first option is the only solution!

Configuring DHCP

DHCP automatically assigns IP addresses to machines that connect to your access point (for more information, see the earlier sidebar "DHCP and NAT").

To enable or disable the DHCP server on the BEFW11S4, click on the DHCP tab. For the DI-714P+, click on the Home tab and then click on the DHCP option.

The BEFW11S4 assigns IP addresses (if the DHCP server is enabled on the router) to all its wireless clients from a default range of 192.168.1.100 to 192.168.1.149 (50 users). The DI-714P+ assigns IP addresses to its clients from a default range of 192.168.0.100 to 192.168.0.199 (customizable).

Disabling the DHCP server on the access point requires all clients that connect to the router to have their own static IP addresses. This makes it slightly harder for unwanted users to connect to your network.

Changing the Administrator Password

A hacker who knows the default password on your access point and who can manage to connect to your network will have full control over your network, and all the other security precautions that you have taken (such as using WEP and disabling DHCP) could come to naught.

To change the Administrator password on the BEFW11S4, click the Password tab. To change it on the DI-714P+, click the Tools tab. I suggest you change the Administrator password frequently.

Disabling SSID Broadcast

By default, the access point will broadcast its SSID to all wireless clients. Anyone in the vicinity with a wireless-enabled computer now knows that you have a wireless network. In order to minimize the chances of allowing uninvited people to connect to your wireless network, it is advisable that you disable the SSID broadcast feature.

To disable the SSID broadcast on the BEFW11S4, select the Setup tab and choose "No" in the "Allow 'Broadcast' SSID to associate?" option.

As of this writing, the DI-714P+ does not have the option to turn off the SSID broadcast.

Viewing the Status of the Access Point

If you need to check on the status of the BEFW11S4, click the Status tab. The Status tab will display information on the following options: LAN and WAN Information such as IP addresses and subnet mask will also be displayed. This is a useful option to troubleshoot network problems that may sometimes occur when you connect the BEFW11S4 to the network.

You can also renew your IP address and see the IP addresses in use by computers on your network (these are assigned by the BEFW11S4's built-in DHCP server) in the Status tab.

If you need to check on the status of the DI-714P+, click the Status tab. The Status tab will display information on the following options: LAN, WAN,

Wireless, and Peripheral. Information such as IP addresses and subnet mask will be displayed. This is a useful option to troubleshoot network problems that may sometimes occur when you connect the DI-714P+ to the network.

SNMP monitoring. SNMP (Simple Network Management Protocol) is a protocol used to monitor network devices. Some access points, such as the DI-714P+, will send SNMP messages (known as *traps*) across the network. You can configure the DI-714P+ to send SNMP messages by clicking Tools and then clicking SNMP.

To receive SNMP messages, you'll need an SNMP monitoring program such as SNMP Trap Watcher (a freeware SNMP trap receiver available from *http:// www.bttsoftware.co.uk/snmptrap.html*). For a comprehensive list of SNMP tools as well as more information about SNMP, see *http://www.snmplink.org/*.

MAC Address Filtering

One of the security measures you can take for your wireless network is to enable MAC address filtering. MAC address filtering ensures that only computers with the specified MAC addresses are allowed (or denied) access to the network. This can prevent wandering users from accessing the network.

 MAC address filtering is not foolproof: using the appropriate utility, a wireless card can assume any MAC address. However, MAC address filtering will prevent users from casually connecting to your access point.

You can use the `ipconfig /all` command to check for the MAC address of your wireless card. Most wireless cards have the MAC address directly printed on it. Figure 5-25 shows the MAC address printed on my Cisco Aironet 350.

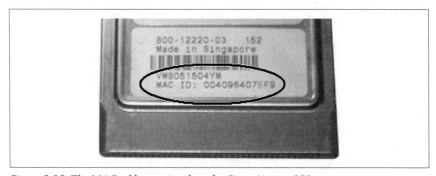

Figure 5-25. The MAC address printed on the Cisco Aironet 350

To enable MAC address filtering on the BEFW11S4:

1. Click on the Advanced tab and then the Wireless tab.
2. Choose the Enable option in the Station Mac Filter section.
3. Click on Edit MAC Filter Setting.
4. Enter the MAC addresses of the wireless card/adapter to which you would like to grant access. If you want to prevent a particular device from connecting, check the Filter checkbox (see Figure 5-26). You can enter up to 32 MAC addresses. (Other routers from Linksys and other vendors may have a different limit.)

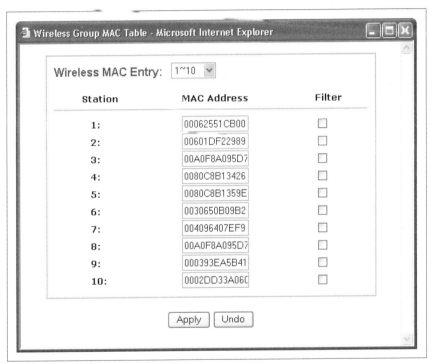

Figure 5-26. Specifying the MAC addresses for enabling wireless access (BEFW11S4)

To enable MAC address filtering on the DI-714P+ (see Figure 5-27):

1. Click on the Advanced tab and then the Filter tab.
2. Choose the MAC Filter option.
3. Choose "Only allow computers with MAC address listed below to access the network".
4. Enter the MAC address of each computer to which you want to allow access and turn on the Enable checkbox.
5. Click the Apply button.

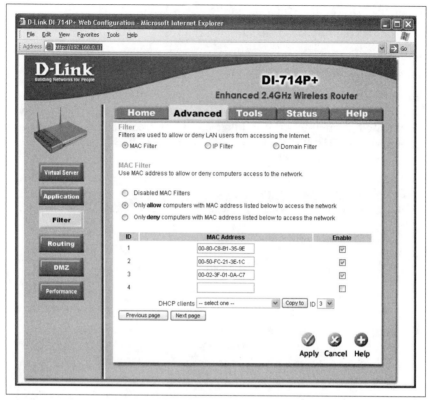

Figure 5-27. Specifying the MAC addresses for enabling wireless access (DI-714P+)

Opening a Port

In some cases, you may want to punch a hole in your firewall to let users on the Internet access a service on one of your computers. For example, you may want to run a public web server on your network. However, when a remote user tries to connect to your public IP address, she'll be stopped dead in her tracks by your access point's firewall.

> Be careful using this option. Even if you only tell a few friends about your web server (or FTP, game, or some other kind of server), malicious hackers will scan your computer on a regular basis (they choose ranges of IP addresses and scan them constantly with automated tools looking for victims), and will be able to tell if the port is open. As soon as they find it, they will begin probing it for vulnerabilities using kits put together by experienced hackers. Unless you are prepared to make daily visits to *http://www.microsoft.com/security/* to check for and act upon security bulletins, you should think twice before punching a hole in your firewall. It's not a matter of whether the hackers will go after you, it's a matter of *when*.

You can configure the access point to accept connections on a particular port and let one of your computers inside your network handle it. For this to be effective, you should configure that computer with a fixed IP address (otherwise, the access point's DHCP server may assign a different IP address each time). If you do this, make sure the fixed IP address is outside the range of DHCP addresses used by your router (see "Configuring DHCP" earlier in this chapter), or you could end up with two computers on your LAN with the same IP address.

To open a port on the BEFW11S4:

1. Click the Advanced tab and select Forwarding.
2. Specify the port or port range, IP address, and whether the port should be open for TCP, UDP, or Both. If in doubt, select Both.
3. Click the Apply button.

To open a port on the DI-714P+:

1. Click the Advanced tab and select Virtual Server.
2. Specify the port or port range (for example, 80–81) and the IP address of the machine running the service, and turn on the Enable checkbox
3. Click the Apply button.

Ad-Hoc Wireless Networking

So far, we have been talking about wireless networks that involve an access point. While this is primarily the way most wireless networks are constructed and used, there are times where you do not have access to an access point and need to simply connect to another computer wirelessly. This mode of wireless connectivity is known as *ad-hoc* mode.

To enable two computers to connect wirelessly without using an access point, you would just need a wireless card/adapter on each computer. Then, take the following steps:

1. Right-click on the Wireless Network connection icon located in the tray and select View Available Wireless Networks. Click on Advanced.
2. The Wireless Network Connection Properties window will appear (see Figure 5-28).
3. Click on Advanced. Select the option "Computer-to-computer (ad hoc) networks only" (see Figure 5-29). (To connect to either an access point or another computer directly, select the option "Any available network (access point preferred)".) Click Close.

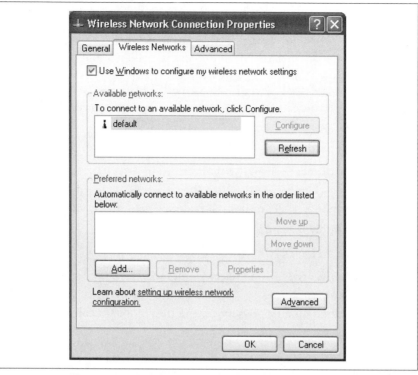

Figure 5-28. Adding a new wireless network

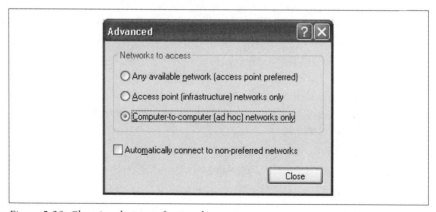

Figure 5-29. Choosing the type of network access

The change in Step 3 will prevent you from connecting to an access point. When you want to go back to connecting to an access point, return to this dialog and reset it to its original value—the default is "Any available network (access point preferred)"

4. Click on Add... and give the ad-hoc wireless network an SSID (see Figure 5-30). Check the option "This is a computer-to-computer (ad hoc) network; wireless access points are not used". Click OK. Click OK again to dismiss the Connection Properties dialog.

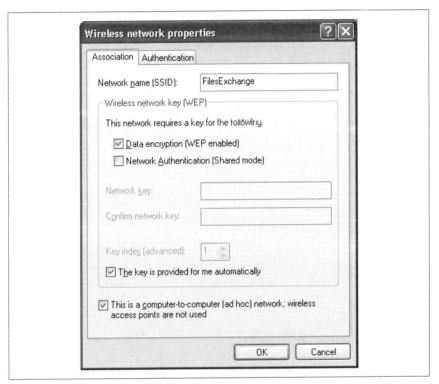

Figure 5-30. Specifying the SSID of the new wireless network

5. On the other computer, right-click on the Wireless Network Connection icon located in the system tray and select View Available Wireless Networks.

6. You should now see the SSID of the ad-hoc network. Select the SSID and enter the key for encryption. (If WEP is enabled, see Figure 5-31. The initiating computer will supply the WEP key.) Both computers should share the same key. Click Connect.

 If you don't see the SSID of the ad-hoc network on the second computer, go into the Advanced settings (as in Figure 5-29) and make sure you have not selected "Access point (infrastructure) networks only." This will prevent all ad-hoc networks from appearing in the list.

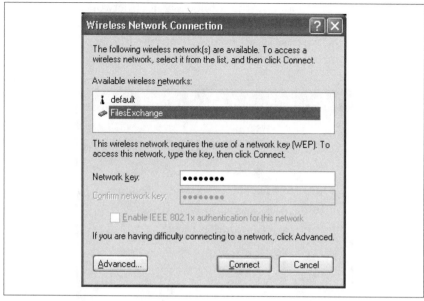

Figure 5-31. Connecting to another computer using ad-hoc mode

7. You should now see that the connection is established (hover the mouse over the Wireless Network Connection icon in the tray). This is shown in Figure 5-32.

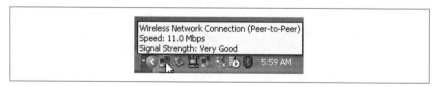

Figure 5-32. Confirming the connection

When you set up an ad-hoc network this way, there is no DHCP server to hand out addresses, but the computers select temporary addresses called *link local addresses*. These are chosen from the Class B subnet (see Chapter 1 for more information on IP addressing) 169.254.0.0/16. To determine the temporary IP addresses, use the *ipconfig* command at the Windows XP Command Prompt.

Note that if you choose to use your own IP address, it will work as well. Also, if you want to share a connection (suppose the first computer is plugged into a broadband connection), you can do so by opening Control Panel → Network and Internet Connections → Network Connections on the first computer, and then:

1. Right-click on the connection that you want to share and select Properties from the context menu. This brings up the Connection Properties dialog.

2. Select the Advanced tab (see Figure 5-33). Check the box labeled Allow other network users to connect through this computer's Internet connection. (If it is already checked, uncheck it, click OK to dismiss the Connection Properties dialog, and start over at step 1.)

Figure 5-33. Sharing an Internet connection over an ad-hoc wireless network

3. To allow other computers to access the Internet connection through the ad-hoc network created on the first computer, select the wireless connection from the Home Networking Connection list and click OK.

Now, when another computer connects to the first computer's ad-hoc network, the first computer will act as a DHCP server and assign it a private network address (if you run into problems, see "Troubleshooting connection sharing" in Chapter 6). The first computer will also perform NAT services to permit the other computer to access the Internet (assuming the shared connection is an Internet connection). In effect, this trick turns a Windows XP machine into an expensive wireless access point!

Setting Up a Wireless Repeater

There are two ways in which you can extend the effective range of a wireless network: put in more wireless access points or use a *wireless repeater*. The former method requires that a wired network connection be available in the location where you want to put the access point. However, if your wired network does not extend to that location, the best solution would be to use a wireless repeater.

At the time of this writing, there aren't many (if any) dedicated wireless repeaters in the market. However, some wireless access points come with a repeating function. The D-Link DWL-900AP+ (see Figure 5-11) is one such model. It supports five modes: Access point, Wireless client, Wireless bridge, Multiple-point bridge, and Repeater.

In this section, I show how to configure the DWL-900AP+ to be used as a wireless repeater. I use it together with the D-Link DI-714P+ (see Figure 5-34).

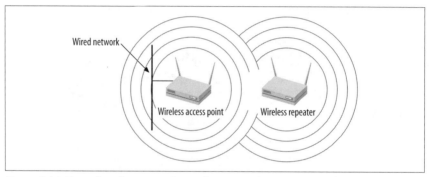

Figure 5-34. Extending the range of a wireless network using a wireless repeater

 The repeating mode of the DWL-900AP+ works only with another D-Link product such as the DI-714P+.

Configuring the DWL-900AP+

First, connect the DWL-900AP+'s LAN port to the LAN port of the DI-714P+. Using a wireless card such as the DWL-650+, connect your Windows XP computer to the DI-714P+.

 You can also use a crossover cable to connect your computer directly to the DWL-900AP+ for configuration.

If you do a site survey, you should be able to see the two SSIDs broadcast by the DI-714P+ (assuming you did not turn off SSID broadcast) and the DWL-900AP+. Connect to the DI-714P+ (or the DWL-900AP+) and use a web browser to invoke the web-based utility of the DWL-900AP+. The default IP address of the DWL-900AP+ is 192.168.0.50.

When prompted for username and password, use "admin" for your user-name and leave the password field empty.

To configure the DWL-900AP+ to act as a repeater, click on the Advanced tab (see Figure 5-35). Check the Repeater option and enter the MAC address of the access point to repeat. Click Apply and the DWL-900AP+ will reboot. You can now disconnect the cable connecting the DWL-900AP+ to the DI-714P+.

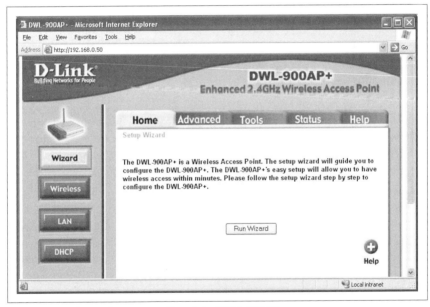

Figure 5-35. The configuration utility of the DWL-900AP+

Perform a site survey again and you should now see only one SSID.

Guidelines for Securing a Wireless Network

Though your new wireless network allows you to have the freedom to surf the Internet anywhere in your house, it also is good news to your neighbors. With your newly set up wireless network, your neighbor can now surf the Internet for free!

Sharing Your Internet Connection with Your Neighbors

Many ISPs prohibit this, and there have been cases of ISPs sending cease-and-desist orders to customers who shared their network access in a large metro area. Another concern is liability: if a malicious hacker uses your Internet connection to attack another site, you'll be among the first people who have to answer questions about the attack. On the other hand, if you want to leave your access point open (such as in a coffee shop), I suggest you give your wireless network a nice friendly SSID and perhaps even put the appropriate Warchalking (*http://www.warchalking.org/*) symbol outside your house!

Unlike a wired network, where you need to have physical access to a network access point, wireless networks extend beyond the four walls of your house.

Most wireless access points and routers provide a web-based configuration program for configuring the wireless access point. The following are some guidelines for securing your wireless network:

Disable SSID broadcast

By default, most wireless access points will broadcast the SSID to all wireless devices. Anyone with a wireless network card can detect the SSID you use and gain access to your network. This brings us to the next point.

Change the default SSID

Most people don't even bother to change the default SSID provided by a wireless access point. If your neighbor knows that you are using a Linksys wireless access point (say, by seeing the boxes you throw away), they could easily try the default SSID. Change it to something less obvious. Note that with some patience and the right tools, discovering an SSID is not difficult. However, changing the default SSID is one step forward in securing your wireless network.

Use MAC address filtering

If you have a small number of users in your wireless network (which is usually the case), you can use MAC address filtering. With MAC address filtering, you find the MAC address of your network card and manually enter this number into your wireless access point. Only MAC addresses that have been registered with the wireless access point are able to gain access to your network. You can usually locate the MAC address of your network card on the device itself.

Change the username and password for the access point's web interface

It is too easy for people to find the default username and password used in wireless access points by consulting a user manual or manufacturer's web site.

Turn off DHCP

If the number of users on the network is small, it is good to turn off DHCP (use static IP addresses instead). Turning off DHCP prevents uninvited users from getting an automatic IP address when they connect to your wireless network. You could instead use static DHCP assignments, where you map an IP address to a specific MAC address. This eliminates the need to do client configuration (giving you all the benefits of the static IP address with configuration centralized on the access point).

Refrain from using the default IP subnet

Most wireless routers use the default 192.168.1.0 network. It is easy for people to guess the IP addresses used and illegally gain access to the network. Also, refrain from using the 192.168.0.0 network address range, since Windows uses this for the private networks it creates with Internet Connection Sharing (ICS).

Use WEP for encryption of packets

If you are concerned about the confidentiality of information transmitted by your wireless network, you may wish to enable WEP encryption. Though WEP has been proven to be nonsecure, it still acts as a deterrent against packet sniffing.

Use something better than WEP

Use a wireless access point that supports something stronger than WEP, such as 802.1X or WPA.

Chapter 4 discusses Wi-Fi security, including 802.1X, in more detail.

Troubleshooting Wi-Fi

Here are some tips to help you if you have problems in getting your USB adapters/cards to work:

- If Windows XP does not automatically install the drivers for your card/adapter, use the drivers provided by the vendor.

- If you did not install the drivers correctly the first time you connected the card to your computer, subsequent connections may cause the card to be unusable. In such situations, go to Control Panel and select Add

Hardware. Select "Yes, I have already connected the hardware" and choose the device that is not working. You will then need to update the driver for your card. Be sure to use the driver from the vendor or download its latest driver from the vendor's web site.

- If you still have trouble in getting a connection to the wireless network, ensure that the wireless card/adapter is enabled. To verify this, right-click on My Network Places and select Properties. Check that the wireless connection is enabled.

- If the wireless network uses WEP for encryption, be sure to enter the WEP key when connecting to the network. If you are using your own wireless network, you can check the WEP key by using the access point's configuration utility (more on this in the section "Configuring an Access Point" earlier in this chapter); otherwise, you need to check with the system administrator for the WEP key.

- If you have a wired connection to the Internet as well as a wireless card/adapter, you can disable the wireless card/adapter by right-clicking on My Network Places and selecting Properties. Right-click on the wireless connection and select Disable. This forces Windows XP to use the wired connection exclusively.

- If you are having trouble with a USB adapter, power down the computer and the USB hub (if you are using one), restore power, and then restart. This can eliminate certain operating conditions that are preventing the adapter from functioning properly by forcing it to completely reinitialize itself when you reapply power.

- If everything appears to be set up correctly, but your network connection frequently drops or slows to a crawl, look for sources of interference. Common sources include microwave ovens and cordless telephones that operate in the 2.4 Ghz range. In general, these will not interfere unless they are very close to your computer or access point, or if they are situated in a direct line of sight (remember that wireless adapters can "see" through walls) between your computer and access point. Also, if you have a whole lot of wireless equipment set up for testing, such as several access points in close proximity, consider relocating them or powering them down when they are not in use. See "Determining wireless coverage with NetStumbler" in Chapter 3 for an easy way to survey your site for signal strength and quality.

CHAPTER SIX

Bluetooth

Named after the Danish King Harald Bluetooth (who ruled approximately from A.D. 940 to 985, and who is reported to have united Denmark and Norway), Bluetooth is a short-range wireless technology with an operating range of 30 feet (10 meters) and a maximum transmission rate of a mere 1 Mbps. Bluetooth is widely touted as a "cable replacement" solution. In the near future, you may not need any cables to connect your keyboard and mouse to the PC, and you may even download your favorite music to your MP3 player wirelessly. In fact, such things are possible today.

Behind the Bluetooth technology is a set of specifications, now under the purview of the Bluetooth Special Interest Group (SIG). The Bluetooth SIG (*http://www.bluetooth.com/*) was spearheaded by Ericsson (the inventor of Bluetooth) and formed in February 2001. The Bluetooth SIG has since grown to have more than 2000 members, comprised of companies such as Ericsson, Nokia, 3Com, Intel, Motorola, Microsoft, and many more.

Bluetooth Standards Today

Bluetooth is a wireless communication technology that is designed for short-range, point-to-point data transfer. Like infrared, Bluetooth is well suited for ad-hoc applications where the presence of a network infrastructure is not available. However, unlike infrared, Bluetooth does not have the limitation of requiring line of sight for communication. Bluetooth uses radio waves in the 2.4 GHz band. Coincidentally, this is also the band used by 802.11b and 802.11g devices. Unfortunately, a lot of domestic appliances also use this 2.4 GHz band, most notably cordless phones and microwave ovens. This means that this 2.4 GHz frequency band (also known as Industrial, Scientific, and Medical, or ISM) is crowded (see the sidebar "Interference Between Bluetooth and Other Devices" in this chapter).

Interference Between Bluetooth and Other Devices

If you are operating an 802.11b (or 802.11g) network together with Bluetooth, Bluetooth performance will take a minor, generally unnoticeable hit. Since both operate in the 2.4 GHz band, interference will cause Bluetooth devices to resend their data. Well, if your father is operating his microwave in the kitchen, that is also going to interfere with your wireless network, whether it is Bluetooth or 802.11. When you are deciding where to put your computers and access points, you need to take this into consideration.

To minimize the impact of interference, Bluetooth uses a technique called *Spread Spectrum Frequency Hopping*. The actual frequency range used by a Bluetooth device is from 2.402–2.480 GHz. Within this range, Bluetooth devices "hop" between the different frequencies with a 1 MHz interval. This essentially gives Bluetooth devices 79 different frequencies to choose from. During a data transfer, the data is divided into packets. Each packet can be sent or received using any of the 79 different frequencies. Per the Bluetooth specification, Bluetooth devices can make up to 1600 hops per second. This essentially reduces the chance that a device will be "jammed" in a fixed frequency. (If the device is experiencing too much interference on the current frequency, you can be sure that it will look for a less busy one in a fraction of a second.)

Piconet

When two Bluetooth devices connect to each other, they create a network called a *piconet*. A piconet contains a *master* and one or more *slaves*. Any device can take the role of a master. The device that initiates the connection (the one that found the other device) is the master. Figure 6-1 shows a piconet containing eight devices (the maximum number allowed in a piconet) with one master and seven slaves.

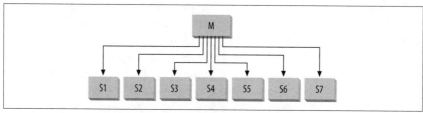

Figure 6-1. A piconet with one master and seven slaves

I mentioned frequency hopping in the previous section. So how do all the devices in the piconet know which frequency to hop to? The master will establish a frequency-hopping scheme and communicate it to all the slaves. All slaves will then follow the frequency sequence set by the master.

Scatternet

When you have more than eight devices to connect, you can form piconets and join them into a larger network called the *scatternet*. A scatternet is made up of up to 10 piconets, giving a total of 80 devices. Figure 6-2 shows a scatternet comprising of two piconets. The individual master in the scatternet serves as a communication bridge between devices in each piconet.

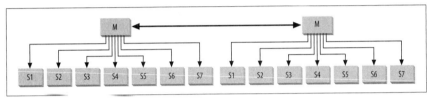

Figure 6-2. A scatternet with two piconets

A device can belong to more than one piconet at any one time. It can also be a master in one piconet as well as a slave in another piconet. But a device cannot be a master of more than one piconet.

When a master is initiating a connection with a slave, it is known as paging. The master selects a new frequency for paging every 312.5 seconds, while the slave(s) selects a frequency to listen at every 1.28 seconds. Eventually, the master and slave devices will encounter a common frequency on which communication can take place.

The frequency hopping nature of Bluetooth devices also helps to enhance the secure communication path between two devices. See the section "Bluetooth Security" in the later part of this chapter for more information.

Bluetooth Device Classes

Bluetooth devices fall into three categories: Class 1, 2, and 3. Most devices in the market today are Class 3. Due to their low power consumption, they operate with a radius of 30 feet (10 meters). For long-range applications, Class 1 devices allow up to 300 feet (100 meters) in operating radius. Table 6-1 shows the range and output of each class.

Table 6-1. Bluetooth device classes

Power class	Range/operating radius	Output power (dBm)
1	300 feet (100m)	20
2	30 feet (10m)	4
3	10cm to 10m	0

What Is dBm?

The unit for output power is dBm, a measure of signal strength in wires and cables at RF and AF frequencies. dBm means "decibels relative to one milliwatt." The output power, *S*, is defined to be:

$$SdBm = 10 \log_{10} P$$

where *P* is the power level in milliwatts (mW). By definition, a 1 mW signal has a level of 0 dBm.

You can freely mix devices of different classes in a piconet or scatternet. However, note the range of each device. For example, Figure 6-3 shows a Class 1 Bluetooth access point with an operating radius of 300 feet. The Class 2 (or 3) Bluetooth adapter is within the access point's range. However, the Class 2 (or 3) device does not have an operating range to reach the access point. Hence the two devices are not able to communicate with each other.

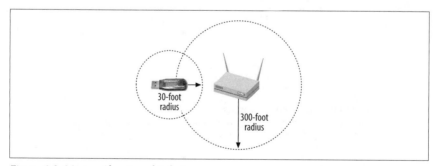

Figure 6-3. Mixing Class 1 and 2 devices

Bluetooth Devices

Just a year ago, Bluetooth devices were a rare species. It was difficult to find Bluetooth add-ons, not to mention Bluetooth-enabled devices. Today, you can find Bluetooth adapters of all shapes and sizes, and with different kinds of interfaces for the various devices. Bluetooth adapters come in the following types of interfaces:

USB
Suitable for desktops and notebooks that have a USB port

Compact Flash (CF)
For use with handheld devices equipped with a CF slot, especially Pocket PCs

PCMCIA
Suitable for notebooks with PCMCIA slots

Secure Digital (SD)
For use with handheld devices equipped with SD slots, such as Pocket PCs and Palm devices

The following sections show some of the Bluetooth devices available in the market today.

USB Adapters and Dongles

The easiest way to add Bluetooth capability to your system is to insert a USB Bluetooth adapter into your USB port. Today, USB Bluetooth adapters come in all shapes and sizes. For as little as $40 you can a get Class 2/3 Bluetooth adapter. For slightly more, you can get a Class 1 adapter that extends the effective communication radius. Figure 6-4 shows the Billionton USB Bluetooth adapter connected to my notebook computer.

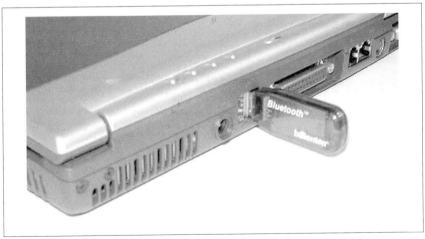

Figure 6-4. The Billionton USB Bluetooth adapter connected to my notebook

Compact Flash

For Personal Digital Assistants (PDAs), a popular format is CF. Many PDAs contain a CF slot for expansion purposes. You can also use the CF Bluetooth cards together with a PCMCIA sleeve and connect it to your notebook computer. CF Bluetooth cards have the advantage of low power consumption, which is useful for battery-powered devices such as PDAs. Figure 6-5 shows the Socket CF Bluetooth adapter.

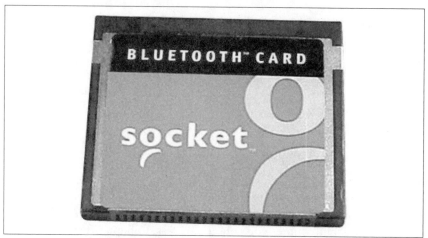

Figure 6-5. Compact Flash Bluetooth Card from Socket

PC Card

Notebook users generally have two choices for Bluetooth capability: a USB Bluetooth adapter or a PCMCIA Bluetooth card. You can also reuse the PCMCIA Bluetooth card on your PDA, if it includes a PCMCIA slot (normally achieved by adding an expansion jacket to the PDA). Figure 6-6 shows the Belkin Bluetooth PC card.

Secure Digital

Toshiba seems to be the only vendor producing the Bluetooth SD (Secure Digital) card (the one used by Palm devices are manufactured by Toshiba). Figure 6-7 shows the Toshiba Bluetooth SD card.

Bluetooth Access Points

Besides 802.11 wireless access points, Bluetooth access points are also becoming common. Figure 6-8 shows the Bluetake BT300 Bluetooth Access Point (AP), which is Bluetooth 1.1 compliant and supports an operating

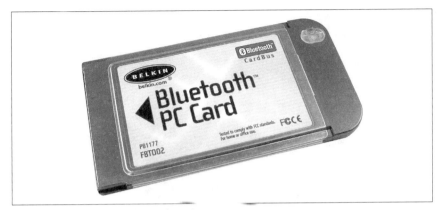

Figure 6-6. A PCMCIA Bluetooth card

Figure 6-7. Bluetooth SD card

range of 100 meters (300 feet). The AP comes with two interfaces: RS232 (standard PC serial adapter) and a 10/100 Base-T Ethernet port. It supports the Bluetooth LAN Access profile (more on this later), operates at a maximum data rate of 1 Mbps, and supports up to seven simultaneous users. I look at how to use a Bluetooth access point for network access later, in the section "Using a Bluetooth Access Point."

Personal Digital Assistants

One of the earliest PDAs to support Bluetooth is HP's (formerly Compaq) iPaq series of Pocket PCs. Starting from the iPaq 3800 series, HP has been building Pocket PCs with the Bluetooth capability built in. Palm has since also built devices that come with the Bluetooth capability built in. The Palm Tungsten T is one such model. Figure 6-9 shows the Palm Tungsten T.

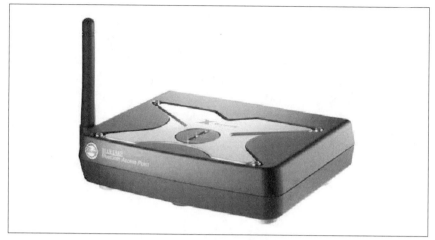

Figure 6-8. The Bluetake BT300 Bluetooth Access Point

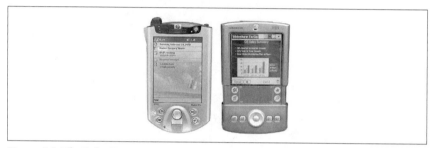

Figure 6-9. The Palm Tungsten T

Cell Phones

Sony Ericsson has been taking the lead in launching Bluetooth-capable mobile phones, which is not surprising since Bluetooth was invented by Ericsson. Starting from the Ericsson T68 to the latest P800, Bluetooth-equipped mobile phones allow you to wirelessly synchronize your calendar and contact database with your Windows XP PC and other devices. Figure 6-10 shows the Sony Ericsson T68i and P800.

Bluetooth Service Profiles

As a consumer technology, Bluetooth needs to be widely supported by vendors to be successful. Interoperability, the ability for different devices (from different manufacturers) to work with one another, is the key factor in securing this broad support (many a technology has been stalled because users were frustrated by incompatibilities and finger-pointing among vendors). In Version 1.1 of the Bluetooth specification (the latest at the time of

Figure 6-10. The Sony Ericsson T68i and the Sony Ericsson P800 (shown with the kind permission of Sony Ericsson; copyright Sony Ericsson 2003)

Ericsson and Sony Ericsson

The original T68 was marketed under the Ericsson brand. It was then that Ericsson and Sony started a joint venture in mobile phone development. Subsequent phones were marketed under the Sony Ericsson label. The Sony Ericsson T68i was an improved version of the T68. In some places, you can convert your T68 to T68i via a firmware upgrade.

this writing), there are 13 profiles. A profile is a description of a particular functionality and how to implement it based on the specification. Bluetooth device manufacturers use these profiles as a guide to implement specific functionality. With this approach, vendors can be sure that their devices will work with current and future Bluetooth products. Let's take a closer look at the 13 profiles defined in Bluetooth 1.1:

Generic Access Profile
The Generic Access Profile (GAP) defines how two Bluetooth devices discover and establish communications between each other. The GAP is the "mother" of all profiles, as it defines modes and procedures used by all the other profiles.

Service Discovery Application Profile
The Service Discovery Application Profile (SDAP) allows Bluetooth devices to query the services available on other Bluetooth devices.

Cordless Telephony Profile
The Cordless Telephony Profile (CTP) defines how a Bluetooth device can be used as a cordless phone.

Intercom Profile

The Intercom Profile defines how two Bluetooth-enabled phones can connect with each other directly without the use of the public telephone network.

Serial Port Profile

The Serial Port Profile defines how two Bluetooth devices can communicate with each other by using virtual serial ports. Using this profile, Bluetooth communication can be treated as just another serial communication.

Headset Profile

The Headset Profile defines how a headset can communicate with a Bluetooth device.

Dial-up Networking Profile

The Dial-up Networking Profile defines how a Bluetooth device can connect to a Bluetooth-enabled modem or mobile phone.

Fax Profile

The Fax Profile defines how a Bluetooth device can connect to a Bluetooth-enabled fax device, such as a fax machine or a fax-enabled mobile phone like the Sony Ericsson T68i.

LAN Access Profile

The LAN Access Profile defines how a Bluetooth-enabled device can connect to a network using PPP (Point-to-Point Protocol).

Generic Object Exchange Profile

The Generic Object Exchange Profile (GOEP) defines a set of protocols used by applications for exchanging objects.

Object Push Profile

The Object Push Profile is used together with the GOEP to send and receive objects, primarily for exchanging electronic business cards.

File Transfer Profile

The File Transfer Profile is used together with the GOEP to transfer files between two Bluetooth devices.

Synchronization Profile

The Synchronization Profile is used together with GOEP to synchronize calendar and address information between two Bluetooth devices, such as a laptop and cell phone.

In this chapter, we will make use of several of the 13 profiles for file transfer, Internet connectivity, etc.

Using a Bluetooth Headset

You can connect a Bluetooth headset to any Bluetooth-enabled device as long as the device supports the Headset profile. For example, I am able to use my Sony Ericsson T610 to connect to the HBH-60 Bluetooth headset (see Figure 6-11).

You can now talk freely without any wires connecting between your headset and your phone. But you have to get used to the occasional stare that passer-bys will give you (the headset looks futuristic and ahead of its time)!

Figure 6-11. The Sony Ericsson T610 and the Bluetooth Headset HBH-30 (shown with the kind permission of Sony Ericsson; copyright Sony Ericsson 2003)

Using Bluetooth in Windows XP

Let's now equip a Windows XP computer with a USB Bluetooth adapter. In this chapter, I illustrate using the Billionton USB Bluetooth adapter (see Figure 6-12).

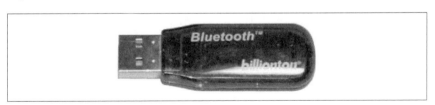

Figure 6-12. The Billionton USB Bluetooth adapter

When you first connect the Bluetooth adapter to your computer, Windows XP detects the new device and prompts for the installation CD. Insert the CD (included with the adapter) and follow the instructions on the screen.

 With other manufacturers' devices, you may need to install the drivers first, and then insert the Bluetooth adapter. Please see the documentation that came with your device for more details. Also, the procedures shown in the following may differ from what you will experience during your own setup. However, the general steps still apply.

1. During the installation stage, you can choose the services that you want your Bluetooth adapter to provide (see Figure 6-13).

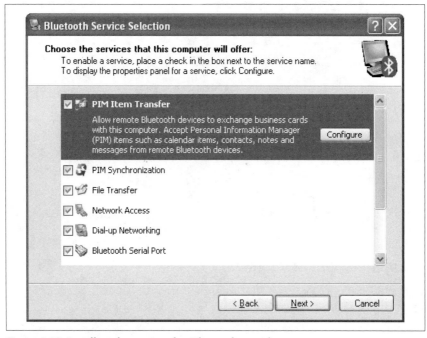

Figure 6-13. Installing the services that Bluetooth provides

2. Once the driver is installed, you should see the Bluetooth icon located in the tray (see Figure 6-14).

Figure 6-14. Locating the Bluetooth icon in the tray

3. Right-click on the Bluetooth icon and you will see a series of options that you can use (see Figure 6-15).

Figure 6-15. The Bluetooth utility

4. When you double-click on the Bluetooth icon in the tray, a window appears, displaying the options as shown in Figure 6-16. We make use of these options in the rest of this chapter.

Figure 6-16. Bluetooth options in My Bluetooth Places

5. Select "View My Bluetooth services" to view the Bluetooth services that your adapter provides (see Figure 6-17)

These services correspond to the Bluetooth profiles that we discussed earlier.

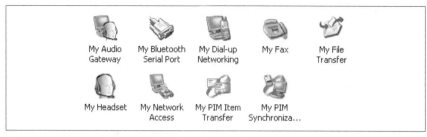

My Audio   My Bluetooth   My Dial-up   My Fax   My File
Gateway   Serial Port   Networking   Transfer

My Headset   My Network   My PIM Item   My PIM
             Access   Transfer   Synchroniza...

Figure 6-17. Bluetooth services that the adapter offers

Who's WIDCOMM and Why Did I Install Their Drivers?

When you installed the Bluetooth software on your PC, you may have noticed the name WIDCOMM at least once, perhaps in the license agreement.

Most Bluetooth adapters use the WIDCOMM Bluetooth Stack driver. WID-COMM (*http://www.widcomm.com*) licenses its software to most Bluetooth manufacturers. Consequently, the installation, configuration, and use of different Bluetooth devices on Windows have a nearly identical look and feel even though Microsoft has not yet (at the time of this writing) released an update to Windows XP to provide native support for Bluetooth. However, Microsoft has released a patch to Original Equipment Manufacturers (OEMs) that supports Bluetooth. This patch is known as QFE (Quick Fix Engineering) 313183. There is a good chance you will find native support for Bluetooth in a future Windows XP service pack. Until then, you will probably use the WIDCOMM drivers supplied by your adapter vendor.

You can download the latest drivers and support software from the adapter vendor's web site. Because each vendor customizes the WIDCOMM software slightly, you should not use drivers from a vendor other than the one who manufactured your Bluetooth adapters.

Connecting to a Pocket PC

You can use Bluetooth to synchronize your Bluetooth-equipped Pocket PC with your computer. If you have a Bluetooth-equipped Pocket PC, you can use the Bluetooth connection as an ActiveSync connection. You can then synchronize your Pocket PC with your computer wirelessly.

> Even if your Pocket PC does not have built-in Bluetooth, you should be able to find a Bluetooth adapter for little more than $100 if your Pocket PC has a Compact Flash slot.

To connect to a Pocket PC, take the following steps:

1. First, you must establish a partnership with your computer through ActiveSync. You need to use a USB sync cable or the cradle that comes with your Pocket PC.

2. If you are using a third-party Bluetooth adapter, you may need to install Bluetooth support software on your Pocket PC. Follow the instructions that came with your Bluetooth adapter to install the Bluetooth software.

3. Next, invoke the Bluetooth Manager on your Pocket PC and search for the host computer running Microsoft ActiveSync. (Some Pocket PC Bluetooth adapters, such as the Socket Bluetooth Connection Kit, do not require this step). Tap on the host computer (LWM 1, in my case) icon and check the ActiveSync Partner checkbox to establish the host computer as an ActiveSync partner (see Figure 6-18).

Figure 6-18. Configuring a Bluetooth device as an ActiveSync partner

4. On the host computer running Microsoft ActiveSync, right-click on the Bluetooth icon in the tray and select Setup → Configuration. Select the Local Services tab and double-click on the Bluetooth Serial Port item (see Figure 6-19). Verify the virtual COM port number used by the Bluetooth serial port. In my case, it is using COM port 4.

5. Next, launch Microsoft ActiveSync and select File → Connection Settings.... Turn on the "Allow serial cable or infrared connection to the

Figure 6-19. Using a virtual COM port for Bluetooth communication

COM port" checkbox and select the COM port number that you used for the Bluetooth serial port. In this case, it is COM port 4 (see Figure 6-20). Click OK.

6. To activate ActiveSync, go to the Today screen of the Pocket PC and tap on the Bluetooth icon (located at the bottom right) and select Start ActiveSync (see Figure 6-21). (Some Bluetooth adapters, such as the Socket Bluetooth Connection Kit, use a menu option titled Bluetooth ActiveSync.)

Your Pocket PC and host computer should start synchronizing now.

Troubleshooting ActiveSync. If you have trouble making the connection, try the following:

Try it with a cable

Be sure that you can use ActiveSync with a USB or serial port connection (whichever the Pocket PC's cradle supports). You must first establish a Standard or Guest partnership between the PC and Pocket PC before you can perform a Bluetooth ActiveSync.

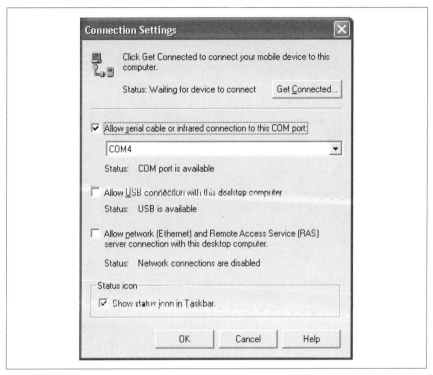

Figure 6-20. Setting a COM port for ActiveSync operation

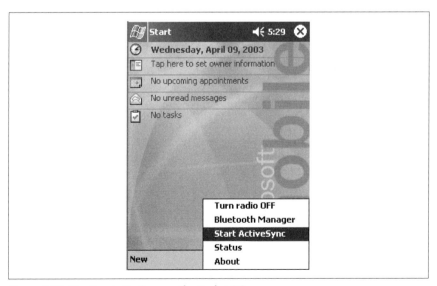

Figure 6-21. Starting ActiveSync on the Pocket PC

Reset your Pocket PC

Many times resetting the Pocket PC will solve the connection problem.

Pair (or bond) your PC and Pocket PC

This ensures that the two can see one another, and avoids the need to search for one another each time you perform an ActiveSync.

Check the ActiveSync Partner box

Ensure that you have turned on the ActiveSync Partner checkbox, as shown in Figure 6-18. Some Bluetooth adapters, such as the Socket Bluetooth Connection Kit, do not require this.

Verify your COM port

Double-check that the COM port used by ActiveSync (right-click on the ActiveSync tray icon and choose Connection Settings) is the same as the one used by your Bluetooth serial port (right-click on the Bluetooth tray icon, choose Setup → Configuration, and then double-click Bluetooth Serial Port in the Local Services tab).

Make sure ActiveSync can see the COM port

If the ActiveSync Connection Settings dialog's Status field (see Figure 6-20) claims that the Bluetooth Serial Port is not available, ActiveSync may not know the serial port exists. If this is the case, click Get Connected in the Connection Settings dialog, and allow ActiveSync to look for your Pocket PC. Make sure that your Bluetooth adapter is connected and active and that your Pocket PC is cradled before you perform this step. This won't cause ActiveSync to locate your Pocket PC over the Bluetooth serial port, but it will let ActiveSync know about all the Bluetooth serial ports available on your PC.

In my testing, I had occasional problems in getting ActiveSync to use the Bluetooth serial port. My best advice is to restart both the computer and the Pocket PC if such a connection problem arises, and try these steps again.

Connecting to a Palm

You can use Bluetooth with Palm Handhelds that have an SDIO slot (such as the Palm m500, m505, m130, or m125 Handhelds) or built-in Bluetooth (such as the Tungsten T). To connect to a Palm, follow these steps:

1. Before you try to connect your Palm and computer over Bluetooth, be sure to get the latest Palm Desktop and Palm Bluetooth software from *http://www.palm.com/software* and install it according to the instructions.

2. Verify that you can perform a HotSync using the Palm cradle or cable before trying to make a Bluetooth connection. (You'll need to do this to install all the Palm Bluetooth software, anyhow.)

3. Remove the Palm from the cradle and, if you are using a Palm with a Bluetooth SDIO adapter, insert the adapter. You should hear a beep when the card is inserted properly.

4. Configure your Palm to use Bluetooth for HotSync:

   a. Tap the Home icon on your Palm to bring up the list of Applications.

   b. Tap the Prefs icon. This brings up the Preferences application.

   c. Tap the menu in the upper-right corner and select Connection. This brings up the Available Connections dialog, shown in Figure 6-22.

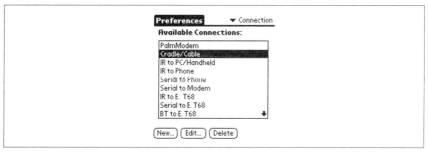

Figure 6-22. Viewing the Palm Connection Preferences

   d. Tap the New button to bring up the Edit Connection dialog. Specify a name, select PC from the Connect To drop-down menu, and choose Bluetooth in the Via drop-down menu (see Figure 6-23).

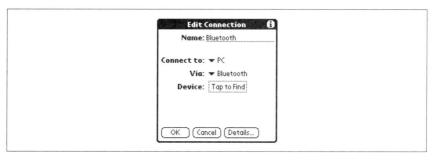

Figure 6-23. Editing the Bluetooth Connection in Preferences

   e. Tap the button labeled Tap to Find. This begins the Bluetooth discovery process (see Figure 6-24).

Figure 6-24. Discovering Bluetooth devices

    f. After a few seconds, the Discovery Results appear. Select your computer from the list. Figure 6-25 shows the discovery results with a Windows XP notebook (CAM-FRANCIUM) and a Mac OS X PowerBook (Brian Jepson's computer). Select your Windows XP computer and tap OK. If the computer is not already paired with the Palm, you'll be asked if you want to add it to your trusted device list. Tap Yes to continue. You'll be asked to enter a passkey on both the Palm and Windows XP computer.

Figure 6-25. Viewing the list of Bluetooth devices

    g. When you have selected the Windows XP PC and paired successfully, you'll be back at the Edit Connection dialog. Click OK to dismiss this dialog.

5. Configure your PC to use Bluetooth for HotSync:

    a. Click the HotSync icon in the system tray and select Local Serial (see Figure 6-26).

    b. Click the HotSync icon in the system tray and select Setup, then select the Local tab (see Figure 6-27).

    c. Select the same COM port used for the Bluetooth Serial Port (right-click on the Bluetooth tray icon, choose Setup → Configuration, and double-click Bluetooth Serial Port in the Local Services tab), and click OK.

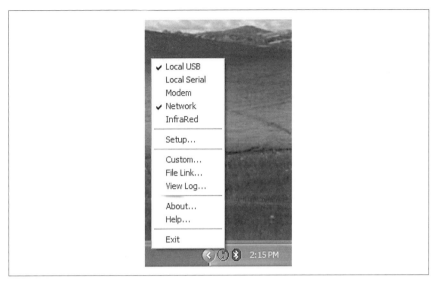

Figure 6-26. Clicking the HotSync system tray icon

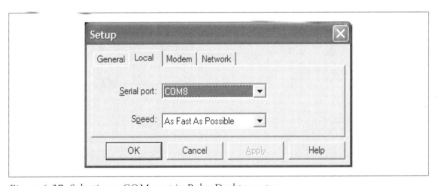

Figure 6-27. Selecting a COM port in Palm Desktop setup

6. Next time you perform a HotSync from your Palm Handheld, choose Bluetooth from the drop-down menu (see Figure 6-28).

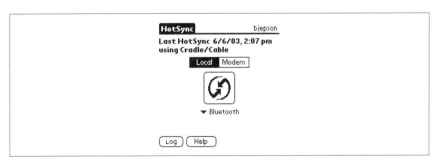

Figure 6-28. Performing a Bluetooth HotSync operation

Connecting to the Internet Through a Mobile Phone

If you have a Bluetooth-equipped mobile phone, such as the Sony Ericsson T68i, you can use it as a modem to connect to the Internet (see "Cellular Networking Price and Performance" in Chapter 8 for more information on pricing). Best of all, with Bluetooth, you can simply leave the phone in your pocket or briefcase and still be able to connect to the Internet (as long as the phone is powered up and your briefcase is within range). In this section, I show you how to connect to the Internet using the Sony Ericsson T68i.

1. First, turn on the Sony Ericsson T68i's Bluetooth radio (press the joystick button and select Connect → Bluetooth → Options → Operation Mode → On) and make the phone discoverable (press the joystick button and select Connect → Bluetooth → Discoverable).

 Turning on the Bluetooth radio on your phone will drain its battery. If you are not using the Bluetooth connection, it is advisable to turn off the Bluetooth radio.

2. In Windows XP, go to My Bluetooth Places and select "View devices in range" (you may also click the Bluetooth menu and select "Search for devices" or open the Entire Bluetooth Neighborhood and press F5). After the discovery process, you should be able to see the Sony Ericsson T68i icon. Right-click on the icon and select Discover Available Services (see Figure 6-29).

Figure 6-29. Discovering the services offered by the T68i

3. The Sony Ericsson T68i supports the services shown in Figure 6-30.

4. To connect to the T68i, right-click on the Dial-up Networking on T68 service and select Connect Dial-up Networking (see Figure 6-31).

5. The phone asks you whether you want to accept the connection request, decline it, or "add to paired." This last step pairs the phone and the PC and performs the connection request. Pairing the phone and the computer ensures that the connection can be established whenever you

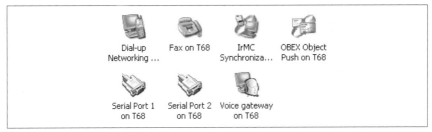

Figure 6-30. Services offered by the T68i

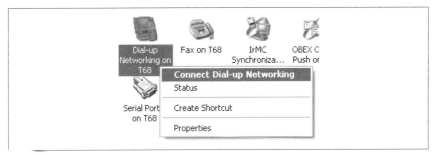

Figure 6-31. Using the Dial-up Networking service on the T68i

need it (even though you have not used the connection for some time). If your phone is not paired, you need to make it discoverable every time you need to use the connection. See the sidebar "Pairing," later in this chapter, for more details.

6. You will be prompted to supply a PIN code to pair up the phone with your computer (see Figure 6-32). You need to enter the same PIN code on your phone.

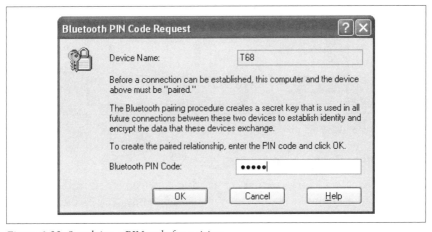

Figure 6-32. Supplying a PIN code for pairing

7. Next, a dialog box will be displayed, prompting you to enter the username, password, and phone number to dial (see Figure 6-33). You can get all this information from your ISP.

 Some ISPs do not require a username or password, just the dialing sequence for the T68i. For example, AT&T Wireless's dial string is *99*CID#, where CID is your connection ID (typically 1, as in *99*1#). This uses the connections defined on your phone (#1 is usually configured by AT&T for your GPRS data connection).

8. Click on the Dial button to complete the connection process (see Figure 6-33).

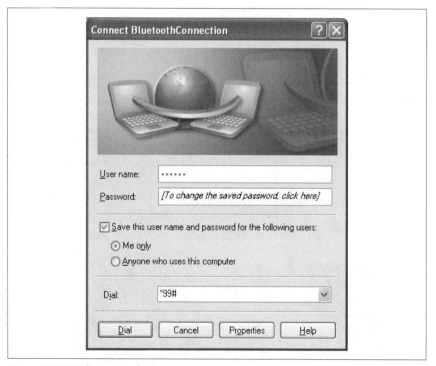

Figure 6-33. Dialing using the T68i

File Transfers Between Computers

Bluetooth was popularly touted as a cable replacement technology. File transfers are a common chore that typically depends on a network cable. (Wi-Fi networking also allows you to create ad-hoc networks for file transfers. See "Ad-Hoc Wireless Networking" in Chapter 5 for more details.)

Pairing

In Bluetooth, you have the option to *pair* two devices. When you pair with a Bluetooth device, this device will be remembered and trusted. The next time you need to use the device, you need not search for it again.

When pairing with a device, the device requesting the pairing will need to supply a PIN code to establish the link. The other device needs the same PIN to complete the pairing process.

You can still use a Bluetooth device without pairing, but you need to search for the device every time you need to use it.

Note that some devices use the word "bonding" to mean pairing.

To pair your computer with a phone (such as the T68):

1. Turn on the Bluetooth radio on T68 and assign a name to it, such as T68.

2. On your Windows XP computer, go to My Bluetooth Places and click on "View devices in range".

3. Right-click on the T68 icon and select Pair Device (see Figure 6-34).

4. Key in the PIN code to be used for pairing on the computer.

5. On the T68, you have three choices: Accept, Add to Paired, or Decline. Select Accept to allow the computer to pair with the phone. Select Add to Paired if you want the phone to add the computer to its paired collection. Select Decline if you do not wish to pair.

If you are pairing your computer with a phone, take care to use numbers only, or else you may have problems keying in alphabetic characters using your phone's PIN code dialog!

Figure 6-34. Pairing with the T68

Bluetooth can be useful in situations when there are no cables or networks available, and you need to transfer files between computers and/or other Bluetooth-enabled devices.

For Bluetooth file transfer, you can typically expect transfer rates ranging from 100 Kbps to a maximum of 750 Kbps. File transfers between computers are generally much faster than between Pocket PCs.

To transfer files between computers, follow these steps:

1. Open up My Bluetooth Places and click on "View devices in range".

2. Figure 6-35 shows that two devices have been found: a Bluetooth access point and another computer (equipped with Bluetooth capability) named Jupiter. Right-click on Jupiter and select Discover Available Services to list the various services that the computer Jupiter provides (see Figure 6-36).

Figure 6-35. Finding the Bluetooth devices nearby

Figure 6-36. Discovering the services offered by another computer

3. Figure 6-37 shows the services that Jupiter provides.

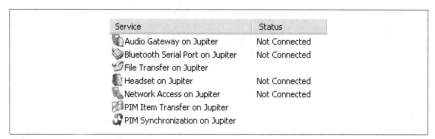

Figure 6-37. Services that Jupiter offers

4. To initiate a file transfer between Jupiter and your computer, double-click on the File Transfer on Jupiter icon (this may also appear as an icon called Public Folder). Depending on the security settings of the remote machine (Jupiter), you may be prompted to enter a PIN code (see Figure 6-38). Once this PIN code is entered, you will also need to enter the same code on Jupiter.

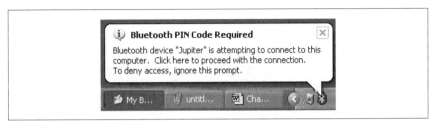

Figure 6-38. Connecting to Jupiter

In some releases of the Bluetooth software, you may need to click on the Bluetooth tray icon to bring up dialogs for PIN codes (clicking the bubble shown in Figure 6-38 will only make it disappear).

5. When connected, you will see Jupiter in My Bluetooth Places as shown in Figure 6-39.

Figure 6-39. You can copy files to Jupiter after connecting

6. You can treat this as just a normal folder. However, when you try to copy files or create a folder on Jupiter, the dialog box shown in Figure 6-40 may appear on Jupiter's screen.

7. There are three permission settings that Jupiter can grant:

For the current task

You allow the operation to be performed once only. Subsequent operations require your explicit consent.

Not Seeing an Authorization Prompt?

Whether you are prompted for authorization depends on the security settings on the remote machine (Jupiter), which you can adjust by right-clicking the Bluetooth tray icon, selecting Setup → Configuration, and then double-clicking the File Transfer in the Local Services tab of the Bluetooth Configuration dialog (check the Authorization box to require Authorization before a transfer).

Figure 6-40. Giving the rights for the remote computer

For the next...x minutes
> You allow operations to be performed within the specified amount of time. After the time limit, all operations require your explicit consent.

Always allow this device to access to my computer's File Transfer service
> You allow all operations to be performed. Subsequent operations do not require your explicit consent.

The files transferred using Bluetooth are stored in the Bluetooth Exchange Folder. To locate this folder, go to My Bluetooth Places in Jupiter and select View My Bluetooth Services. Right-click on My File Transfer and select Bluetooth Exchange Folder (see Figure 6-41).

If this option is not available, go to the Bluetooth configuration, right-click the Bluetooth tray icon, select Setup → Configuration, and go to the Information Exchange tab. The folder listed as My Shared Directory (see Figure 6-42) contains files transferred to your computer.

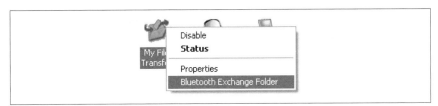

Figure 6-41. Viewing the Bluetooth Exchange Folder

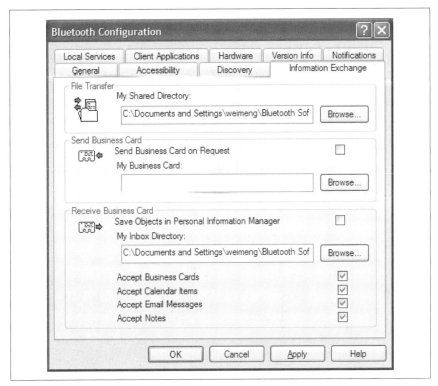

Figure 6-42. Viewing the location of the Bluetooth exchange folder

Sharing an Internet Connection Using Bluetooth

Using Bluetooth, two computers can share an Internet connection (see Figure 6-43). Assuming that one computer (equipped with Bluetooth) is connected to the Internet via an Ethernet (or Wi-Fi) connection, another computer that is also equipped with Bluetooth can establish a Bluetooth connection with it and share the connection to the Internet.

On the computer providing the Internet connection. To share an Internet connection and set it up on the computer that is providing the connection, follow the steps described in the list shown next.

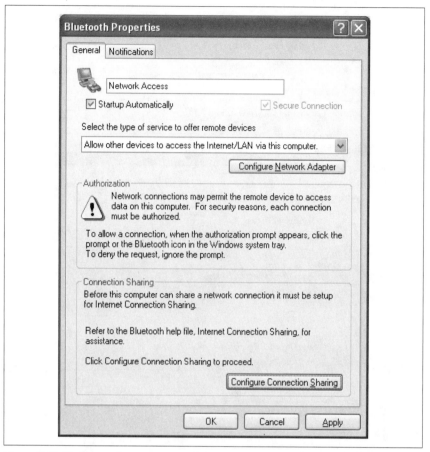

Figure 6-43. Sharing an Internet connection

1. Go to My Bluetooth Places and select View My Bluetooth Services (or navigate to My Bluetooth Places → My Device in Windows Explorer). Right-click on Network Access and select Properties.

2. Change the type of service to offer remote devices to "Allow other devices to access the Internet/LAN via this computer" (see Figure 6-43). If your Bluetooth software does not offer this option, you may proceed to the next step without changing this setting.

3. Click on the Configure Connection Sharing button. The Network connections window will be displayed. (If your Bluetooth software does not support this option, you can also bring up this window by opening Windows Explorer → My Computer → Control Panel → Network and Internet Connections → Network Connections.) Select the network connection that you want to share with other computers that connect to

you via Bluetooth. For example, you may have an Ethernet connection for Internet access, or you may have a wireless connection. Right-click on the connection of your choice and select Properties.

4. To enable Internet connection sharing, click on the Advanced tab (see Figure 6-44). Turn on the "Allow other network users to connect through this computer's Internet connection" checkbox (if it is already checked, uncheck it, click OK to dismiss the Connection Properties dialog, and start over at step 3). In the drop-down list box, select Bluetooth Network. (If this connection is not available, look for the network connection listed as Bluetooth LAN Access Server in Network connections, which may be named something cryptic such as Local Area Connection 7.) Click the OK button.

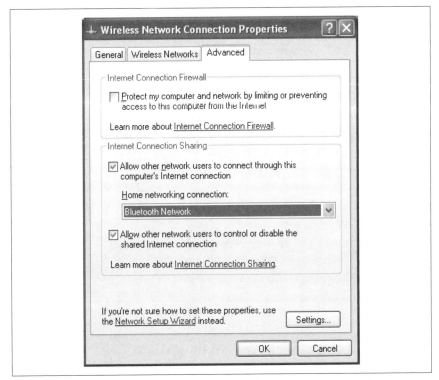

Figure 6-44. Configuring the connection to be used for Internet connection sharing

On the computer using the shared Internet connection. To share an Internet connection and set it up on the computer that is using the connection, follow the steps described in the list shown next.

1. On the computer using the shared Internet connection, go to My Blue-tooth Places and select "View devices in range". Select the computer providing the Internet connection and right-click on the Network Access Service. Select Connect to Network Access Point, as shown in Figure 6-45. You may be prompted for a user ID and password, in which case you must use a user ID and password that are valid on the remote computer.

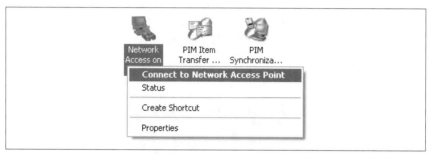

Figure 6-45. Connecting to the shared Internet connection

2. On the host computer providing the Internet connection, a dialog box may prompt for permission to share the network (see Figure 6-46), depending on that computer's security settings.

Figure 6-46. Giving permission to the remote computer for Internet sharing

3. Click on the OK button to complete the connection.

That's it! Both computers should now be able to connect to the Internet by using the host's Internet connection.

Troubleshooting connection sharing. One common problem in sharing an Internet computer on a host computer is IP address conflict. One easy way to prevent this error is to use DHCP to assign IP addresses. On the computer using the shared Internet connection, ensure that you obtain an IP address dynamically using DHCP. This can be done by right-clicking on My Network Places and selecting Properties. Choose the Bluetooth Network icon and configure the property of Internet Protocol (TCP/IP) to obtain an IP address automatically.

Here are some troubleshooting tips:

Make sure you have an IP address

Use `ipconfig` to check whether an IP address has been allocated to your computer. If you do not have an IP address, then the connection has not been established correctly.

Check your connection

Use `ping` to verify that you can reach other computers. Open a Windows XP Command Prompt, and type `ping` *computername*, as in `ping jupiter` (always try the computer that's sharing the Internet connection first). Then you might want to try to ping a remote host, such as *www. oreilly.com*.

Check your name servers

Use `nslookup` to resolve the hostname of a remote computer, such as *www.oreilly.com*. This can help you to verify whether you are able to connect to the Internet.

Make sure the host computer is still connected

Go to the computer that's sharing its Internet connection, and check to see whether it's lost its connection to the Internet.

Bluetooth Printing

Printing wirelessly is another popular use of Bluetooth technology. This is especially useful in a small office environment where many coworkers need to share a single printer. Instead of buying a more expensive network printer, you can purchase a Bluetooth printer adapter and connect it to your printer. Users can then print wirelessly using Bluetooth.

Figure 6-47 shows the Bluetake BT200 Bluetooth printer adapter (other vendors offering Bluetooth printer adapters include MPI Tech and Anycom), which connects to the parallel port on your printer. It is a Class 2 Bluetooth device and supports the Serial Port Profile.

In the following, I show you how I use the BT200 to connect to my HP 5L laser printer.

1. First, establish a connection between your computer and the printer using a parallel cable. Once you can print correctly using the parallel cable, power down the computer and printer, disconnect the parallel cable, and connect the Bluetooth printer adapter to the printer.

Figure 6-47. The Bluetake BT200 Bluetooth Printer Adapter

 The Bluetake Bluetooth printer adapter that I used in this chapter connects only to a parallel port printer. But if you have a USB printer, you can get the Bluetooth printer adapter for it from MPI Tech at *http://www.mpitech.com/*.

2. Right-click on the Bluetooth icon in the System Tray and select Advanced Configuration. Click on the Client Applications tab (see Figure 6-48).

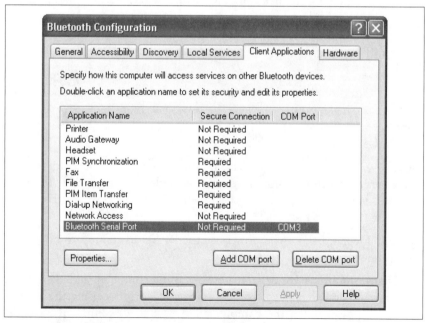

Figure 6-48. Verifying the COM port used as a serial port

3. Confirm the COM port used for the Bluetooth Serial Port. In my case, the port number is COM3. We will use COM3 to connect to the printer using Bluetooth. Also, double-click on Bluetooth Serial Port to ensure that the Secure Connection checkbox is unchecked.

4. Since our printer is going to connect to this virtual COM3, we need to configure our printer to connect to this COM port, not the parallel port. Go to Start → Settings → Printers and Faxes. Locate your printer and right-click on it. Select Properties. Turn off the LPT port checkbox and turn on the COM3 checkbox. Click OK (see Figure 6-49).

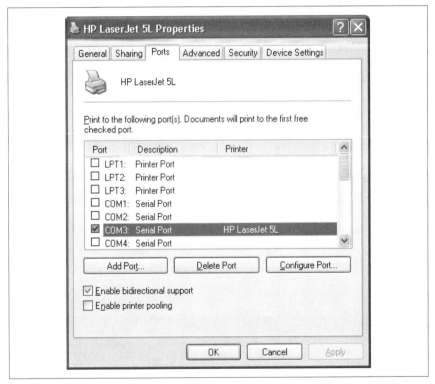

Figure 6-49. Configuring the printer to print to a virtual COM port

5. Next, go to My Bluetooth Places and select Bluetooth Setup Wizard.

6. In the Bluetooth Setup window, select "I know the service I want to use and I want to find a Bluetooth device that provides that service" (see Figure 6-50). Click Next.

7. In the next window, select Bluetooth Serial Port (see Figure 6-51) and click Next.

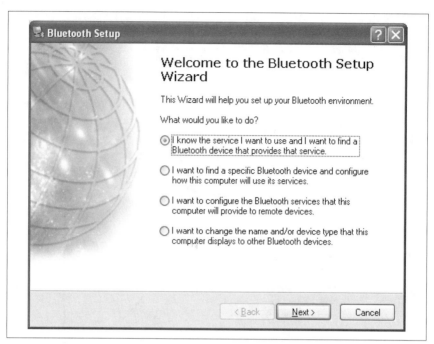

Figure 6-50. Using the Bluetooth setup wizard to set up the printer

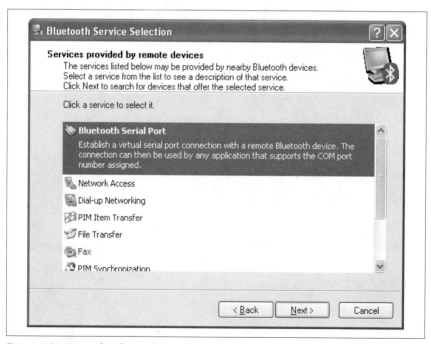

Figure 6-51. Using the Bluetooth serial port to connect to the printer

8. Bluetooth will now search for other Bluetooth devices. Select "Show printers, cameras and scanners" from the drop-down list (see Figure 6-52). You should be able to find a device call BT200. Select it and click Next.

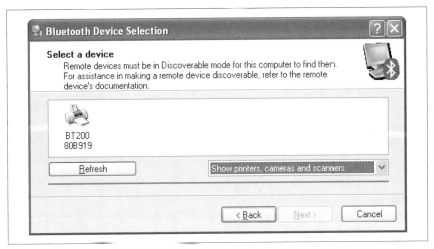

Figure 6-52. Locating the printer

9. Finally, a Cable Replacement icon will be created in My Bluetooth Places. Click Configure to confirm the settings for this connection (see Figure 6-53).

That's it! You can now print normally to your printer, and Bluetooth will perform its magic wirelessly in the background.

Troubleshooting Bluetooth printing. Here are two solutions to common problems in getting your printer to print wirelessly:

• Ensure that your printer is configured to print to the Bluetooth Serial Port.

• Because different vendors have different setup instructions, follow the installation instructions provided by the vendor.

Bluetooth LAN

Like Wi-Fi access points, Bluetooth access points are increasingly popular. Using a Bluetooth access point is similar to using a Wi-Fi access point—connect the access point to a wired network and you can wirelessly connect your Bluetooth devices to the Internet.

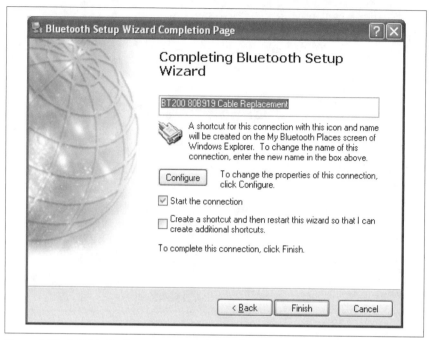

Figure 6-53. A Cable Replacement icon to link to the printer

Using a Bluetooth Access Point

In following steps, I illustrate the use of a Bluetooth access point by using the Bluetake BT300 Bluetooth Access Point (AP).

Connecting to the Bluetooth access point. To connect to the access point, follow these steps:

1. First, connect your Bluetooth access point to your router/hub (you can also connect it directly to your ADSL/DSL/cable modem). Power up your Bluetooth access point, go to My Bluetooth Places, and search for the Bluetooth access point.

2. When the access point is found, right-click on the icon and select Discover Available Services, as shown in Figure 6-54.

3. The Bluetooth access point supports the LAN access using PPP service. Right-click on the LAN Access icon and select Connect to Network Access Point, as shown in Figure 6-55.

> By default, the Bluetooth access point has a static IP address of 1.1.1.1. You can configure it to obtain its address from a DHCP server. I discuss this in more detail in the later section "Configuring the Bluetooth access point."

Figure 6-54. Discovering the services that the Bluetooth access point provides

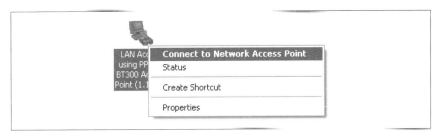

Figure 6-55. Connecting to the Bluetooth access point

4. You should then see a dialog prompting you to enter your username and password. Simply leave these boxes empty and click on Connect, as shown in Figure 6-56.

You should now be able to connect to the Internet.

Configuring the Bluetooth access point. By default, the connection to the Bluetooth access point is set at 115200 bps. You should set it to the maximum of 921600 bps. To do so, right-click on My Network Places and select Properties. Then, right-click on BluetoothNullConnection and select Properties. Under the General tab, click on the Configure... button. This is shown in Figure 6-57.

One problem that you need to look out for is when you connect the Bluetooth access point to a router. You need to assign an IP address to the access point before you can connect to it using the Internet. To do so, once you are connected to the access point, use a web browser and configure the access point (see Figure 6-58) using the URL *http://1.1.1.1:5000*. The default username and password for the Bluetake access point are BT and access_point, respectively. Check the documentation that comes with your Bluetooth access point.

Click on the *Configuration* link to configure the access point.

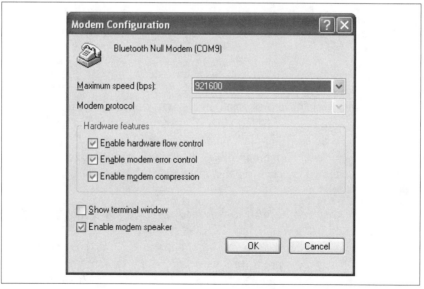

Figure 6-56. Click on Connect to log on to the Bluetooth access point

Figure 6-57. Changing the maximum transfer speed of the Bluetooth access point

For those using an ADSL/DSL modem, choose the PPPoE option (see Figure 6-59). For cable modem users, choose DHCP. (If you are not sure whether your Internet connection uses DHCP or PPPoE, contact your ISP.) There are also three security options available—levels 1 to 3. For security

Figure 6-58. Configuring the Bluetake access point

level 3, you need to supply a PIN code. You can also optionally enable data encryption. But doing so will effectively reduce the data transfer rate.

Network type:

⦿ Fixed IP address   ○ PPPoE (for ADSL)   ○ DHCP

Security level:

[level 1 ▾]   PIN code: [_____]

Encryption: ☐ Enable data encryption

[OK]

Figure 6-59. Configuring the network type and security for the access point

If you use security level 3, you will be prompted to enter the PIN code when your computer connects to the access point (shown in Figure 6-60).

Figure 6-60. Prompt from the access point when security level 3 is selected

Click on the prompt and enter the PIN code, as shown in Figure 6-61.

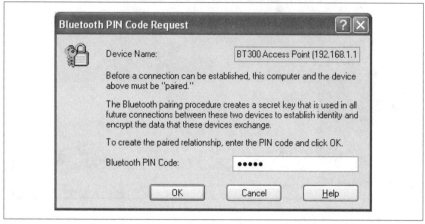

Figure 6-61. Entering a PIN code to connect to the Bluetooth access point

You can now test your connection by using a web browser and see whether it can connect to a web site.

Testing the Connection

I tested the connection using my two USB Bluetooth adapters—a Class 1 Bluetake USB adapter and a Class 3 Billionton USB adapter. Performance was comparable between the two except that the Class 1 Bluetake Bluetooth adapter is able to operate at a longer distance. I was able to surf the Web comfortably without any noticeable difference. One thing I gathered is that Bluetooth works best if there is a lot of free space for the radio waves to reach you. I tried locating the AP in a closed room (with concrete walls) and accessing the network two rooms away, and the signal dropped to a rather weak level. I did, however, maintain the connection, although it was slow. With Bluetooth, you can connect up to seven devices to the AP, a number that should be sufficient for most home use. Using Bluetooth for LAN communications is useful for small devices (such as Palm and Pocket PC) because Bluetooth generally uses less power than 802.11b.

Bluetooth Security

You saw in Chapter 4 that wireless security is always a concern to administrators. You have also seen the flaws inherent in 802.11's WEP security. What about Bluetooth? Is it any more secure than 802.11?

The short and quick answer is no, Bluetooth is no more secure than 802.11. Because Bluetooth is often used in short-distance communications, its security aspects aren't well publicized, but it has certainly had its share of security woes.

In Windows XP, to enable secure Bluetooth communication using encryption, right-click on the Bluetooth icon located in the Tray and select Advanced Configuration. Click on the Local Services tab, and select the services that you want to enable encryption.

For example, you can select the Bluetooth Serial Port service and click on Properties. Check the Secure Connection checkbox to enable encryption (see Figure 6-62).

Figure 6-62. Enabling encryption for the Bluetooth serial port

In this and following sections, I explain how security is implemented in Bluetooth and some of the security concerns of which you need to be aware.

As shown in Figure 6-63, Bluetooth has three security modes:

1. Security Mode 1 doesn't provide security. A Bluetooth device in this mode allows any device to connect to it. This is useful for applications that don't explicitly require security, such as the exchange of business cards.

2. Security Mode 2 works at the service level. It is secured at the application layer (in other words, it is secured after a connection has been established). An application can be written to allow access to certain services (by another device) while restricting certain services.

3. Security Mode 3 works at the link level. It is secured before a connection is established between two devices. The use of a link key (or PIN code, as seen in earlier sections) is used to authenticate the identity of another device.

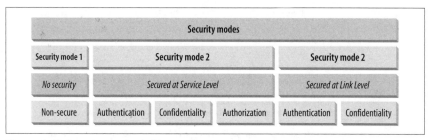

Figure 6-63. Security modes in Bluetooth

Authentication

Authentication verifies the identity of a device. First, some definitions are in order: a *claimant* is the device that needs to be authenticated, and a *verifier* is one that verifies the identity of the claimant.

Here is the sequence of the authentication process:

1. The user enters a PIN code (on both the claimant and the verifier).

2. The two devices use the PIN code to generate a 128-bit link key.

3. The claimant transmits its address (a 48-bit address, similar to the MAC address of a wireless card) to the verifier.

4. The verifier transmits a 128-bit random challenge to the claimant.

5. Both the claimant and the verifier use the SAFER+ algorithm (Secure and Fast Encryption Routine) to generate a 32-bit *authentication response*. The SAFER+ algorithm takes in as input the link key, claimant's address, and the 128-bit random challenge.

6. The claimant transmits the 32-bit authentication response to the verifier, which then compares it with its own. If the two authentication responses are identical, the authentication is successful; otherwise, it fails.

When an authentication fails, a Bluetooth device has to wait for an interval of time before it can be authenticated again. This is a security measure against hackers using a rapid trial-and-error approach.

Figure 6-64 shows the authentication process.

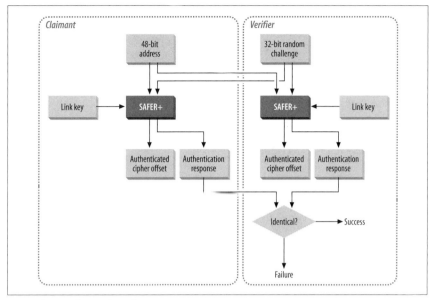

Figure 6-64. Bluetooth authentication process

Encryption

Encryption protects the confidentiality of data transmitted between two Bluetooth devices. The Bluetooth specification supports three modes of encryption:

Encryption Mode 1
No packets are encrypted in this mode.

Encryption Mode 2
Data transmitted to a specific device is encrypted, but data broadcast to multiple devices is not.

Encryption Mode 3
All the data transmitted is encrypted.

Here is the sequence for the encryption:

1. A Key Generator generates an encryption key using as input the 96-bit Authenticated Cipher Offset (a result returned by the earlier authentication process), the Link key, and the 32-bit random challenge. The size of the encryption key ranges from 8 to 128 bits, and is negotiated between the master and the slave.

2. A key stream is produced using a cryptographic algorithm based on LFSR (Linear Feedback Shift Registers). The LFSR takes in as input the encryption key generated, the master's address, the 32-bit random challenge, and the slot number to be used for the current packet.

The key stream produced for each packet is different, since the slot number varies with each packet (due to frequency hopping). In a way, this is a security feature of Bluetooth.

3. The key stream produced is then XOR'ed with the plaintext, which is then transmitted to the master.

Figure 6-65 illustrates the process of encryption.

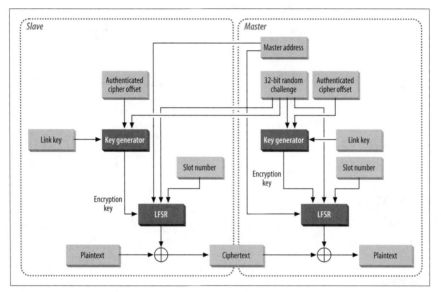

Figure 6-65. Bluetooth encryption process

Bluetooth Security Concerns

A detailed survey of Bluetooth security issues is beyond the scope of this book. However, based on what I have discussed, the following are some of the concerns with regards to Bluetooth security:

* The PIN code used for establishing a link is usually short and thus easy to guess. Longer PIN codes could be used. However, users normally prefer a shorter PIN code for convenience.

* Distribution of PIN codes in a large network is difficult. Fortunately, this is not a major concern, as Bluetooth is commonly used for ad-hoc networking.

* The 32-bit random challenge may generate numbers that follow a certain pattern. This reduces the effectiveness of the encryption.

* Authentication is only at the device level; user-level authentication must be explicitly implemented.

As Bluetooth is a relatively new standard, the Bluetooth specifications are still undergoing changes. Over time, you can expect to see more security measures being put in place. At the moment, it is appropriate to apply some of the techniques used for securing network communications on some types of Bluetooth connections. For example, you could use a VPN or SSH (see Chapter 4) in conjunction with a Bluetooth network connection.

CHAPTER SEVEN

Infrared

If you have ever used a remote control, you have used infrared technology. Infrared is a wireless communication technology that makes use of the invisible spectrum of light that is just beyond red in the visible spectrum. It's suitable for applications that require short-range, point-to-point data transfer. Because it uses light, line of sight is a prerequisite for using infrared. Despite this limitation, infrared is widely used in household equipment and is increasingly popular in devices such as digital cameras, PDAs, and notebook computers.

Founded in 1993 as a nonprofit organization, the Infrared Data Association (IrDA) is an international organization that creates and promotes interoperable, low-cost infrared data interconnection standards that allow users to point one device at another and have it just work. The Infrared Data Association standards support a broad range of appliances, computing, and communications devices.

 The term IrDA is typically used to refer to the protocols for infrared communications, not exclusively to the nonprofit body.

In this chapter, I take a look at Windows XP's support for infrared and show how you can make use of it for your daily tasks.

IrDA in More Detail

There are currently four versions of IrDA; their differences are mainly in the transfer speed. They are:

Serial Infrared (SIR)
    This is the original standard with a transfer speed of up to 115 Kbps.

Medium Infrared (MIR)
    Improved transfer speed of 1.152 Mbps. Not widely implemented.

Fast Infrared (FIR)
Speed of up to 4 Mbps. Most new computers implement this standard. Windows 2000 and XP support this implementation.

Very Fast Infrared (VFIR)
Speed of up to 16 Mbps. Not widely implemented yet.

Future versions of the IrDA will boost speed up to 50 Mbps.

When two devices with two different IrDA implementations communicate with each other, they will both step down to the lower transfer speed.

In terms of operating range, infrared devices can communicate up to one or two meters. Depending on the implementation, if a device uses a lower power version, the range can be stepped down to a mere 20 to 30 cm. This is crucial for low-power devices.

All data packets exchanged are protected using a Cyclic Redundancy Check (CRC), which uses a number derived from the transmitted data to verify its integrity. CRC-16 is used for speeds up to 1.152 Mbs and CRC-32 is used for speeds up to 4 Mbs. The IrDA also defines a bi-directional communication for infrared communications.

IrDA Adapters

If you use a notebook computer, you most likely have an infrared port. Most notebook computers come with an infrared port built in; look at the back of your notebook and you should be able to find it. The port is usually a dark red color. Figure 7-1 shows the infrared port at the back of an HP notebook.

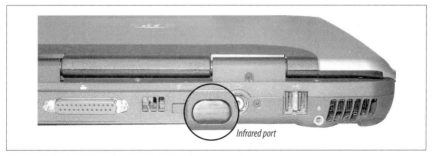

Figure 7-1. An infrared port at the back of a notebook computer

USB Infrared Adapter

It is rare to find an infrared port on a desktop computer. Most desktop manufacturers have not incorporated infrared functionality into their design, mainly because of the lack of demand for it. However, you can add infrared functionality into your desktop by purchasing a relatively cheap (under $50) infrared adapter. Figure 7-2 shows a USB infrared adapter. To use it, simply plug the adapter into the USB port and Windows XP will automatically recognize and install the driver for the device.

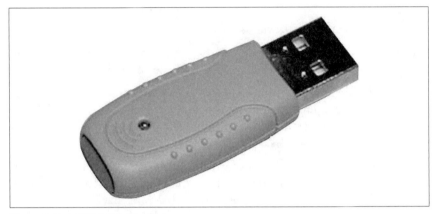

Figure 7-2. A USB infrared adapter

You can verify that your Windows XP computer supports infrared functionality by going to Start → Settings → Control Panel → System. Go to the Hardware tab and click on Device Manager. If you can locate the icon named Infrared devices (see Figure 7-3), then your computer is capable of infrared functionality. If you cannot locate this icon, ensure that you really have an infrared port or connect your infrared adapter again.

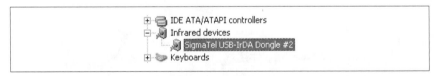

Figure 7-3. Infrared support in Windows XP

Using IrDA in Windows XP

Windows XP supports the IrDA protocols, providing connectivity to the Internet and to other networks. Using Windows XP support for infrared communication, you can connect to the Internet using a dial-up infrared modem or connect to another computer through point-to-point connection. You can also connect to the Internet through a computer and a network access point.

The advantage of using Windows XP for infrared communication is transparency to the end user.

> For dial-up networking, when an infrared device is within range of another device, Windows XP will automatically install the necessary device (such as an infrared modem). Two kernel-mode drivers (*IrCOMM* and *IrEnum*) and an *.inf* file (*Mdmirmdm.inf*) provide this functionality.

For LAN access networking, Windows XP uses the IrNET protocol, which uses the Point-To-Point (PPP) protocol over the infrared link for network access.

Infrared File Transfer

Imagine that you are at a conference and would like to send a couple of files to someone that you have just met. There might not be a network available, and it is unlikely that you lug a serial cable with you when you travel. If both of you are using notebook computers, the best solution is to use infrared to send the files.

When two computers are within communicating range of each other (with the infrared port of each computer pointing at each other), Windows XP will automatically activate the irFTP application, which is found in the *C:\ Windows\system32* directory. The irFTP application allows two computers to exchange files using infrared. You can use this utility at the command prompt. To see a list of options, enter the command irftp /h.

> Exchanging files between computers using infrared is similar to doing so with a Pocket PC; this is demonstrated in the following section.

Computer to Pocket PC

Most Pocket PCs contain a built-in infrared port for communicating with the outside world. Using the infrared port, you can transfer files from the Pocket PC to the computer (and vice versa) without using a cable. Figure 7-4 shows the iPaq 3870 with the infrared port located at the top.

When you align the infrared ports of both the Pocket PC and your computer, Windows XP will inform you that a Pocket PC is nearby (see Figure 7-5).

The Send files to another computer icon (a shortcut to the irFTP application) also appear on your desktop (see Figure 7-6).

Figure 7-4. The infrared port located at the top of the iPaq 3870

Figure 7-5. Discovering a nearby computer using infrared

Figure 7-6. The shortcut to the irFTP application

You can double-click on the icon shown in Figure 7-6 to send files to your Pocket PC (see Figure 7-7).

Select the file that you want to send and click on the Send button.

Pocket PC to Computer

To send files from the Pocket PC to the computer, go to File Explorer on the Pocket PC, then tap and hold on to the file that you want to send, to bring up the context menu. Select Beam File... as shown in Figure 7-8.

On your computer, you will receive a prompt seeking your permission to accept the file. Click on Yes to receive the file, or click Cancel to reject it (see Figure 7-9).

On the receiving computer's end, you need to click on the infrared icon located in the tray to accept the incoming file. Windows XP does not always automatically display a window for that. If you do not click on the icon manually, the sending computer continues to wait for a reply.

Figure 7-7. Sending files using infrared

You can configure the default directory for file transfer by right-clicking on the infrared icon in the tray (shown in Figure 7-10) and selecting Properties from the pop-up menu.

This brings up the Wireless Link dialog, shown in Figure 7-11.

If you did not configure a default location for received files, the incoming file(s) will be saved on the desktop.

ActiveSync

Another use of infrared is synchronizing your Pocket PC with your computer. With ActiveSync, you can use infrared to connect to your Pocket PC without a syncing cradle or cable.

To use infrared for ActiveSync, launch Microsoft ActiveSync on your computer and click File → Connection Settings.... Turn on the "Allow serial cable or infrared connection to this COM port" checkbox (see Figure 7-12) and click OK.

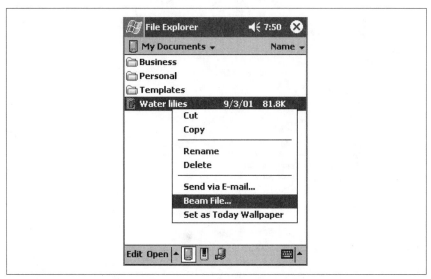

Figure 7-8. Sending a file on a Pocket PC using infrared

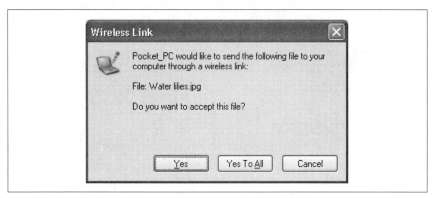

Figure 7-9. Requesting permission to accept or reject a file

Figure 7-10. The infrared icon in the Tray

Align the infrared port of the Pocket PC to that of the computer and on the Pocket PC, launch ActiveSync and select Tools → Connect via IR... (see Figure 7-13).

Microsoft ActiveSync should now start connecting to the Pocket PC.

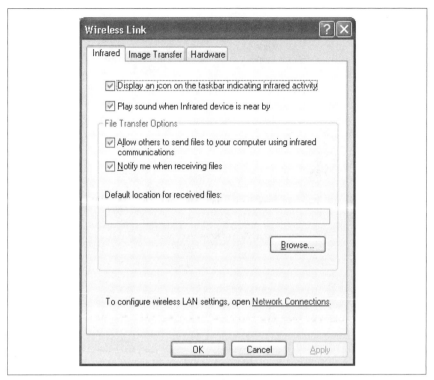

Figure 7-11. Configuring the properties for infrared communication

Connecting to the Internet Via Infrared

In this section, I illustrate how you can connect to the Internet using a mobile phone. The phone used in this example is the Nokia 6610 (see Figure 7-14), which supports GPRS data access.

 For more information on GPRS, please refer to Chapter 8.

Invoke the Infrared option (go to Menu → Connectivity → Infrared) on your mobile phone.

Align the phone's infrared port (see Figure 7-15) to that of your computer's.

Windows XP will automatically detect the Nokia 6610 (see Figure 7-16).

Windows XP will also query the device for the services that it provides. In the case of the Nokia 6610, a classic phone (with modem capability) is

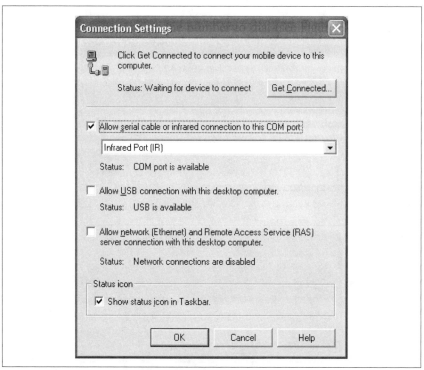

Figure 7-12. Configuring Microsoft ActiveSync for infrared communication

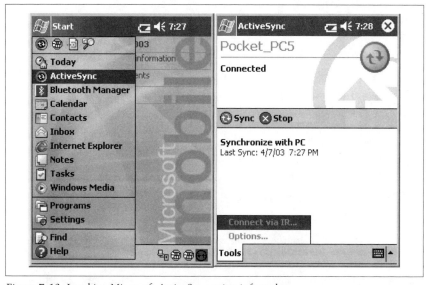

Figure 7-13. Invoking Microsoft ActiveSync using infrared

Figure 7-14. The Nokia 6610

Figure 7-15. The infrared port for the Nokia 6610

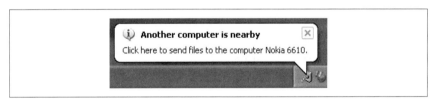

Figure 7-16. Detecting the Nokia 6610

detected, and Windows XP automatically installs a standard modem over the IR link (see Figure 7-17).

You are now ready to set up your computer to use the Nokia 6610 as a modem:

1. Right-click on My Network Places and select Properties.
2. Select Create a New Connection.

Figure 7-17. Installing a standard modem over the IR link for the Nokia 6610

3. A wizard will appear to help you set up the connection. Choose the following options in each dialog:

- Connect to the Internet
- Set up My Connection manually
- Connect using a dial-up modem

A list of available modems will be displayed (see Figure 7-18). Choose the standard modem over the IR link.

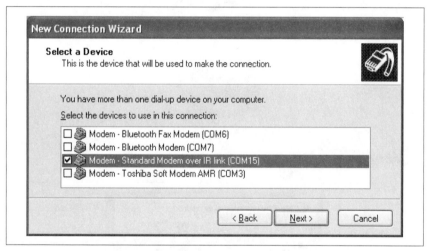

Figure 7-18. Selecting the IR modem for dial-up access

You will be prompted to enter the ISP name, username, and password. You need to obtain all this information from your ISP.

Finally, turn on the "Add a shortcut to this connection to my desktop" checkbox. Double-click on the connection icon, and a connection window appears as shown in Figure 7-19.

Sharing Internet Connection Using Infrared

Using an infrared connection, two computers can share an Internet connection. Assuming that one computer with an infrared port is connected to the

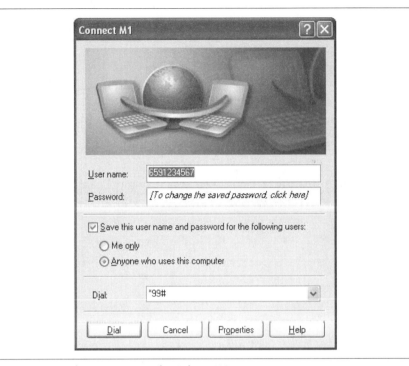

Figure 7-19. Dial-up access using the Nokia 6610

Internet via an Ethernet connection, another computer that is also equipped with an infrared port can establish a connection with it and share the connection to the Internet.

On the computer that is connected to the Internet:

1. Right-click on My Network Places and select Properties.

2. Select Create a New Connection.

3. Select Set up an Advanced Connection and click Next. The Advanced Connection Options dialog appears.

4. Select Accept Incoming Connections and click Next. The Devices for Incoming Connections dialog appears.

5. Choose the devices for the connection. In this case, you should choose the Infrared Port (IRDA3-0); see Figure 7-20. Click Next. The Incoming Virtual Private Network (VPN) Connection dialog appears.

6. Select Do Not Allow Virtual Private Connections and click Next. The User Permissions dialog appears.

7. Select the user accounts that should be allowed to connect to this computer (see Figure 7-21).

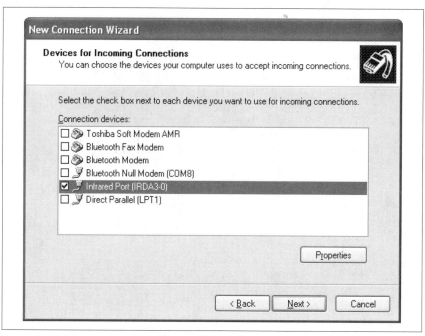

Figure 7-20. Selecting the infrared port for Internet sharing

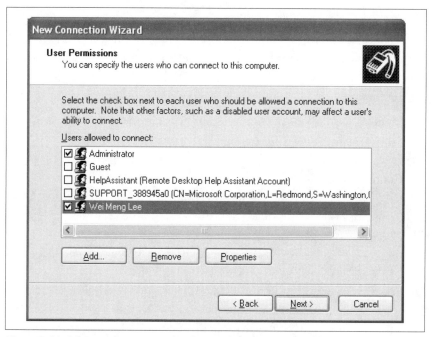

Figure 7-21. Selecting the accounts for sharing the Internet connection

8. Finally, select the protocols to be installed for the connection. Accept the default settings (see Figure 7-22).

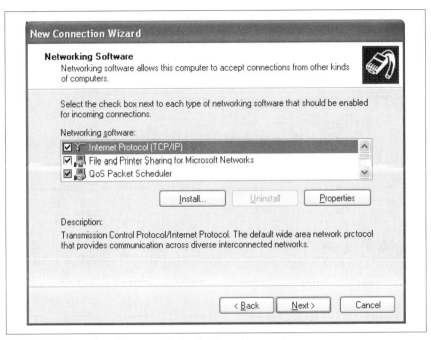

Figure 7-22. Installing the protocols for the shared connection

That's it! Your computer is now ready to accept incoming connections.

On the computer that is going to use the shared Internet connection, you need to perform these same steps. However, in step 4, instead of configuring an incoming connection, select the option "Connect directly to another computer" (see Figure 7-23). Click Next. The "Host or Guest?" dialog appears. Do the following:

1. Select Guest and click Next. The Connection Name dialog appears.

2. Give the host computer a name and click Next. The Select a Device dialog appears.

3. Select the device to be used for the connection. In this case, use the Infrared port (IRDA3-0); see Figure 7-24. Click on Next to complete the installation.

4. You now see the connection window (see Figure 7-25). Enter the username and password that corresponds to the account name that you selected for access in the last section.

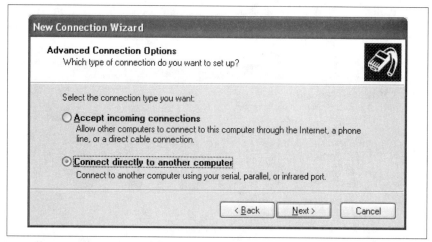

Figure 7-23. Creating a connection to the host computer

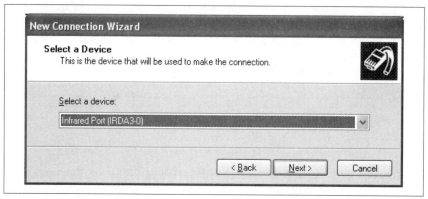

Figure 7-24. Selecting an infrared port to be used for connection

You can now connect to the Internet using the infrared port. Subsequently, you can connect to the Internet by aligning the infrared ports of the two computers and double-clicking on the icon bearing the remote host computer's name (located in the Network Connections window).

 You may need to configure your web browser for Internet access. For example, if the host computer requires you to specify a proxy server for Internet access, you also need to specify it in your web browser settings.

Infrared Security

Unlike Bluetooth and 802.11, Infrared requires an unobstructed line of sight in order for two devices to communicate with each other. It also has a much

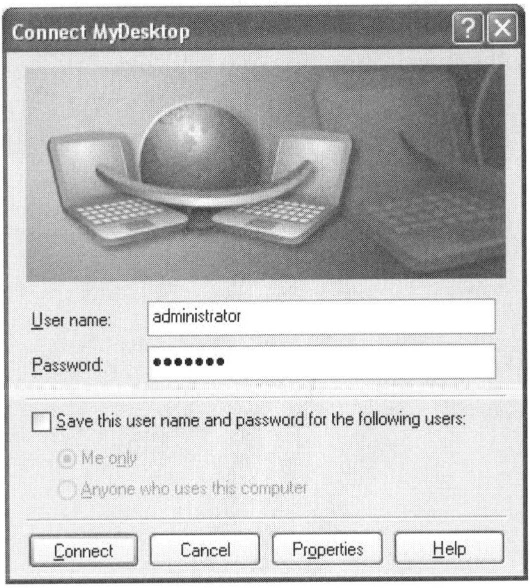

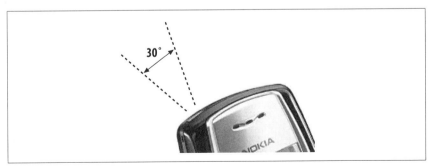

Figure 7-25. Connecting to the host computer

smaller operating range, compared to the other two. For these reasons, Infrared does not provide any security mechanism at the link level; instead, applications must implement their own security measures at a higher protocol level.

To better understand the security risk of Infrared, let's look at some characteristics of it. An infrared connection operates at a range of 0 to 1 meter, with peak intensity within a 30 degree cone (see Figure 7-26). With more power, a longer operating range is possible with a reduction in transfer speed. In addition, an infrared connection requires a visual line of sight (LOS) in order to work. In other words, there must be no direct obstruction between the two communicating devices.

Figure 7-26. The 30 degree cone for peak power intensity of an infrared port

Considering that infrared communications operate at such a short range, it is quite difficult for an attacker to eavesdrop without being noticed (or completely breaking the connection).

Cellular Networking

In theory, cellular networking offers the ultimate unwired experience: network connectivity as long as you are in range of a cell tower. In practice, it's much less than its promise, but it's still getting better every day. Most unwired power users employ a combination of Wi-Fi hotspots and cellular networking to satisfy their lust for bandwidth.

Cellular Networking Price and Performance

Cellular networking offers the following downstream speeds (for activities such as receiving email, downloading files via FTP, and surfing the Web):

- 19.2 Kbps on first generation (1G) networks. CDPD (Cellular Digital Packet Data) is a once-popular 1G service that cellular providers are hoping to phase out.

- 50–70 Kbps on early third-generation (3G) networks (often referred to as 2.5G), sometimes peaking to 144 Kbps. General Packet Radio Services (GPRS) is the leading 2.5G service. AT&T Wireless uses GPRS for its mMode consumer-oriented data plans and its Mobile Internet business-oriented data plans. T-Mobile uses GPRS for its T-Mobile Internet data plans.

- 144 Kbps and higher on 3G networks. CDMA2000, Enhanced Data GSM Environment (EDGE), and Wideband CDMA (WCDMA) are emerging 3G technologies. The first phase of CDMA2000 is 1x Radio Transmission Technology (1xRTT); it is used by Verizon's Express Network and Sprint's PCS Vision. At the time of this writing, EDGE is not widely available, but is reported to have been quietly deployed by AT&T Wireless and Cingular.

Upstream speeds (for activities such as sending email, using FTP to upload files, and uploading documents to web sites) are generally less than the download speeds, anywhere from 9.6 Kbps to about one-half the downstream speed.

One of the fundamental limits on cellular networking is the price of data. Typical packages offer a bucket of data with coverage charged per kilobyte over the limit. Table 8-1 shows some examples based on current U.S. pricing.

Table 8-1. 1G, 2G, and 3G pricing

Quantity	1G	2.5G and 3G
Unlimited	$40-$60/month	$80 or more per month for 1xRTT service. At the time of this writing, T-Mobile is the only GPRS provider advertising unlimited data plans ($29.99/month).
5 Mb	n/a	$15–$20 per month
20 Mb	n/a	$35–$55 per month

A busy user can blow through 20 megabytes in a couple hours of web surfing and email. So heavy users should opt for an unlimited pricing plan, or carefully plan out their usage to take advantage of (free, if possible) Wi-Fi hotspots and use the cellular service only when absolutely necessary (such as sending out an urgent email while sitting on a runway).

Even with a data allotment that you're comfortable with, service can be spotty, though coverage is most comprehensive in densely populated areas (especially Europe and Asia). However, in a densely populated area such as New York City, buildings can interfere with the signals, and many simultaneous users can limit the performance of the network in a given area.

As tempting as it is to chalk up performance problems to early adoption doldrums, the old maxim still stands: let the buyer beware. If you knowingly purchase poor service in the hopes that it will improve over time, keep in mind that there is no guarantee that it will. When in doubt, seek the opinions of others; the Usenet hierarchy *alt.cellular.** has many newsgroups devoted to specific carriers where you can read about peoples' experiences (you can read and post to these newsgroups through Google Groups at *http://groups.google.com*). Be sure to get service from a provider who offers a complete refund, no questions asked, within a reasonable trial time (some providers offer 15 days, which is too little, so try pressuring the sales person for a 30-day trial).

GPRS

General Packet Radio Service (GPRS) is a data service that supplements other data services such as Circuit Switched Data (CSD, used for data and fax calls on GSM networks) and Short Message Service (SMS). The design of GPRS was informed by the fact that wireless data communications are bursty in nature. That is, the data is not sent in one long stream, but rather in short bursts. Traditional use of CSD such as the Wireless Application Protocol (WAP) for data transfer requires establishing connections between two communicating parties, which occupies bandwidth even when not transmitting data. With GPRS, data is sent as packets as and when required. This feature allows devices to stay connected all the time, and eliminates the need to establish a connection and stay connected within the entire duration. This allows service providers to bill customers based on the data transferred and not the connection time.

In this section, I take a closer look at how GPRS works, as well as some of the devices that you can use on the road.

GSM Networks and GPRS

GPRS is a packet-switched service built on the existing Global System for Mobile (GSM) communication voice network. GSM was primarily designed for voice services.

A GSM channel contains eight *timeslots* (a portion of time allocated to transmit data), with each timeslot dedicated to each circuit-switched call. Traditionally, when using Circuit Switched Data (CSD)—which is explained in more detail in the sidebar "What Is CSD/HSCSD?" later in this chapter—you can only use a maximum of one timeslot. With GPRS, timeslots can be assigned dynamically, and you can use more than one single timeslot. This results in increased throughput, which was was previously not possible with CSD. Also, because timeslots are only allocated when required, more users can be supported at any one time.

GSM networks have more worldwide coverage than any other cellular technologies, such as CDMA and PDC (Personal Digital Cellular) used in Japan. In Asia and Europe, the frequencies used for GSM are 900 and 1800 MHz. In North America, it is 1900 MHz. Phones that support these three frequencies are known as tri-band phones. Examples of tri-band phones are the Sony Ericsson T68i and the Nokia 6610.

GPRS and 3G

3G wireless (or Third-Generation wireless) is an initiative to provide enhanced voice, text, and data services. The main draw of 3G networks is the vastly increased data transfer rate of between 384 Kbps and 2 Mbps. With these speed improvements, applications that support real-time video and high-quality multimedia elements can be deployed.

However, deploying 3G networks is not an overnight affair. This requires heavy investment from wireless carriers as well as from telephone and modem manufacturers. In the midst of waiting for the next generation wireless networks, GPRS bridges the gap between the current 2G networks (such as GSM or TDMA) and the forthcoming 3G networks. As such, GPRS is commonly known as 2.5G.

3G networks will likely be using W-CDMA (Wideband Code Division Multiple Access) technology, which is backed by industry giants like Nokia and Ericsson. In Europe, UMTS (Universal Mobile Telephone Service) has been adopted as a 3G network.

How GPRS Works

GPRS uses multiple timeslots for sending data. In theory, GPRS can use up to eight timeslots, but physical constraints (such as the number of users currently on the network as well as the coverage quality) have placed the number to a maximum of five, with one or two timeslots reserved for upstream communications (leaving three or four for downloads).

There are altogether four encoding schemes used in a GPRS network. Table 8-2 shows these and their data rate per timeslot as well as their maximum data speed for eight timeslots. The encoding scheme to be used is determined by the service provider and depends on factors such as the quality of the channel (the radio link between the GPRS device and the base station). CS-1 has the highest reliability (but the lowest data rate) and CS-4 has the least reliability (but the highest data rate).

Table 8-2. Coding schemes used in GPRS

Channel coding scheme	Data rate per timeslot	Maximum data speed with eight timeslots
CS-1	9.05 Kbps	72.4 Kbps
CS-2	13.4 Kbps	107.2 Kbps
CS-3	15.6 Kbps	124.8 Kbps
CS-4	21.4 Kbps	171.2 Kbps

Each GPRS device also belongs to a particular class. A class determines the number of timeslots used for downloading and uploading. The manufacturer of the GPRS device determines the class of a device.

Table 8-3 shows the 29 classes for GPRS devices. Each class has a designated number of timeslots used for downloading and uploading. The maximum slots column lists the maximum number of timeslots that a device can use simultaneously for downloads and uploads.

Table 8-3. GPRS device classes

Class	Download	Upload	Maximum slots
1	1	1	2
2	2	1	3
3	2	2	3
4	3	1	4
5	2	2	4
6	3	2	4
7	3	3	5
8	4	1	5
9	3	2	5
10	4	2	5
11	4	3	5
12	4	4	5
13	3	3	unlimited
14	4	4	unlimited
15	5	5	unlimited
16	6	6	unlimited
17	7	7	unlimited
18	8	8	unlimited
19	6	2	unlimited
20	6	3	unlimited
21	6	4	unlimited
22	6	4	unlimited
23	6	6	unlimited
24	8	2	unlimited
25	8	3	unlimited
26	8	4	unlimited
27	8	4	unlimited
28	8	6	unlimited
29	8	8	unlimited

To put these numbers into perspective, let's take an example and illustrate how all these numbers determine the throughput of a GPRS device.

The Nokia D211 GPRS PC card is a Class 6 device (I talk more about this card in the next section). This means that it has 3 timeslots allocated for downloads (sometimes referred as 3+2, for 3 timeslots for downloads and 2 timeslots for uploads). If I use the Nokia D211 in Singapore and my ISP supports the CS-2 coding scheme, then the maximum downstream speed of the D211 is (13.4 Kbps × 3), giving a maximum download speed of 40.2 Kbps.

 In practice, the theoretical data rate of 40.2 Kbps is not achievable due to real-world conditions such as signal interference and protocol overhead.

GPRS devices fall into three categories:

Class A
> Class A devices can connect to GSM and GPRS services simultaneously, and both can work at the same time. This is the ideal communication device.

Class B
> Class B devices can connect to either GSM or GPRS services (or both at the same time). But only one can work at a time. An example of Class B device is a GPRS-enabled mobile phone such as the Ericsson T68i. You may be using the GPRS service and suddenly a voice call comes in. You can use either the voice service or the GPRS service, but not the two simultaneously. Most mobile phones today are Class B devices.

Class C
> Class C devices can connect to GSM or GPRS services (but not both at the same time). The user must manually switch between the two services. An example of Class C device is the Nokia D211 GPRS card. You need to manually switch between GSM and GPRS services.

GPRS Devices

GPRS devices are commonly called "GPRS terminals." These come in different shapes and sizes, but can be grouped into the following categories:

- GPRS phones
- GPRS modems
- GPRS modules

A constantly updated list of GPRS terminals can be found at *http://www. gsmworld.com/technology/gprs/terminals.shtml*.

GPRS phones. Many new mobile phones support GPRS for data access. Two such phones are the Sony Ericsson T68i and the Nokia 6610 (see Figure 8-1).

Figure 8-1. The Sony Ericsson T68i and the Nokia 6610 (shown with the kind permission of Sony Ericsson; copyright Sony Ericsson 2003)

Using a GPRS-enabled phone, you can access WAP applications on your mobile phone. You can also connect your Windows XP computer to your mobile phone (through Bluetooth or infrared) and use it as a GPRS modem. You can then access the Internet.

What Is a SIM Card?

A SIM is a smart card placed inside a GSM phone that identifies the user account to the network. It handles tasks such as authentication and acts as data storage for user data such as phone numbers, Short Message Service (SMS) messages, and network information. Figure 8-2 shows a SIM card inserted into a mobile phone.

A SIM card may also contain applications that run on the phone.

Chapters 6 and 7 discuss how you can use Bluetooth and infrared connections to connect to your GPRS-enabled phone for Internet access.

GPRS modem. For dedicated data access, you can use a GPRS modem. This is usually a PC card that allows you to make data calls. To use a GPRS modem, you need to insert your Subscriber Identity Module (SIM) card into your phone or PCMCIA card; it also requires a subscription to the data service provided by your ISP. The Sierra Wireless Aircard® 750 (see Figure 8-3) is a GPRS modem card that supports GPRS data access in addition to GSM voice calls and SMS messages.

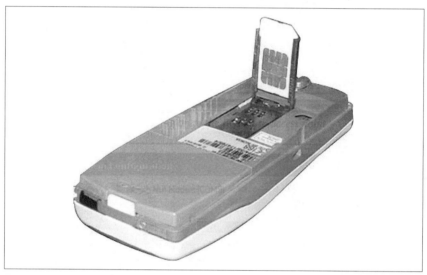

Figure 8-2. A SIM card inserted into a mobile phone

GPRS modules. GPRS modules are commonly used by vertical application developers such as value-added service providers and equipment manufacturers.

The Sony Ericsson GM47/GM48 (see Figure 8-4) is a radio device that can be incorporated into other devices such as a vending machine, an alarm monitoring system, etc. It allows systems developers to build GPRS (and GSM) functionality into their systems.

The Sony Ericsson GM29 (see Figure 8-5) uses the GM47/GM48 hardware module. The GM29 is marketed as a GSM/GPRS modem. It is a Class B (4+1) device with an RS232 connection.

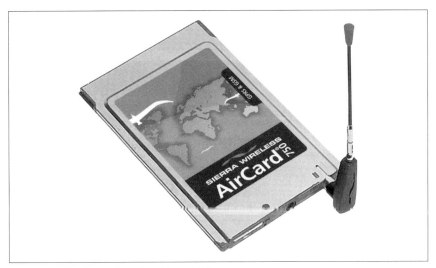

Figure 8-3. The Sierra Wireless Aircard 750

Figure 8-4. The Sony Ericsson GM47/GM48 GSM module (shown with the kind permission of Sony Ericsson; copyright Sony Ericsson 2003)

Figure 8-5. The Sony Ericsson GM29 GSM/GPRS modem (shown with the kind permission of Sony Ericsson; copyright Sony Ericsson 2003)

Using a GPRS/GSM PCMCIA Card

The Nokia D211 (see Figure 8-6) and D311 are multimode radio cards (PCMCIA cards) that support GPRS, CSD (Circuit Switched Data), HSCSD (High Speed Circuit Switched Data; D211 only), and 802.11b networks. It is slightly longer than a conventional wireless card and combines the best of both worlds: allowing you to access a wireless network as well as connect to the Internet through GPRS when a wireless network is not available. The beauty of the D211 is that all these functionalities are integrated in one card, which makes it ideal for road warriors. The only downside is that you cannot make voice calls using the D211; otherwise, the card would be perfect.

Figure 8-6. The Nokia D211

 Both T-Mobile and AT&T Wireless offer the Sierra Wireless AirCard 750; although it does not support Wi-Fi, it is voice capable.

Installing the drivers and support software. Installing the Nokia D211 is a straightforward procedure:

1. Install the provided software using the installation CD.
2. Insert the card into a PCMCIA slot on your notebook.
3. Windows XP will search for the appropriate drivers using wizards. Select the option "Install the software automatically," and then select "Continue Anyway" to continue with the installation.
4. When the software is installed, you should be able to see the icon of the Nokia software located in the Tray (see Figure 8-7).
5. Double-click on the icon in the Tray to invoke the Nokia D211 Manager (see Figure 8-8).
6. The Nokia D211 Manager contains three main functions: Profiles, Settings, and Tools. The Profiles function allows you to configure the various settings for Wi-Fi, GSM and GPRS access. The Settings function

What Is CSD/HSCSD?

Circuit Switched Data (CSD) is the regular way to transfer data using a circuit switching technique. It is like making a voice call between two parties—you have to establish a connection first. Once you are connected, you can then start talking. With CSD, charges are based on the time you spend connected with the other party. CSD allows data rate of 9.6 Kbps to 14.4 Kbps.

High Speed Circuit Switched Data (HSCSD) is the same as CSD except that its data rate is much higher—up to 43.2 Kbps is possible.

Compared to CSD, GPRS charges are usually billed based on the data actually transferred, not by connection time. However, GPRS service is generally quite limited in comparison to companion voice plans. For example, it would not be unusual to get 500 voice minutes per month (if you pick the right promotion, you could double that) for $40 but to get only 20 megabytes of data for another $40. So, when you run out of megabytes at GPRS speeds (40 Kbps or more), you can switch over to dialing into a dial-up ISP at your workplace at CSD speeds, at which point you start using up your voice minutes (and whatever fees your ISP charges). Note that some U.S. providers do not permit CSD calls. For example, as of this writing, it is impossible to initiate a CSD call with AT&T Wireless's 2.5G service.

Figure 8-7. The Nokia software icon located in the Tray

allows you to fine-tune the various settings for GSM, WLAN, and Security. The Tools function contains a diagnostics utility as well as log information, etc.

 In this chapter, I use the D211 to illustrate the configuration process. You should substitute the D211 with the D311 if you reside in the U.S.

Configuring WLAN access. The Nokia D211 and D311 support 802.11b wireless network access. Let's configure the card for wireless access now. Here are the steps:

1. Ensure that you have selected the Profiles function from the Nokia D211 Manager.

2. Click on the Modify tab.

3. Click on New....

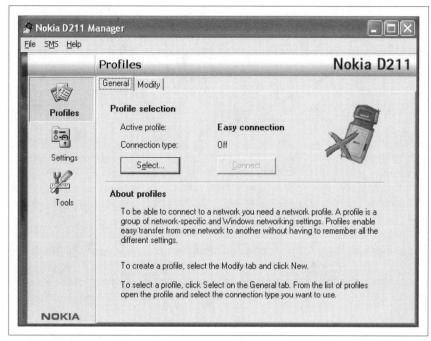

Figure 8-8. The Nokia D211 Manager

D211 Versus D311

Nokia has two GPRS radio cards: D211 and D311. These two models are almost similar, except that the D211 is sold (and usable) in Europe and Asia, whereas the D311 is sold in the U.S.

The D211 supports dual band EGSM (Enhanced GSM) and operates at frequencies of 900/1800 MHz. The D311 supports dual band GSM and operates at frequencies of 850/1900 MHz. The D211 supports CSD and HSCSD while the D311 supports only CSD.

The most significant difference between the D211 and the D311 is in the data rate. D211 supports up to 43.2 Kbps (using HSCSD; a maximum 40.2 Kbps. when using GPRS) while the D311 only supports up to 14.4 Kbps (using CSD; a maximum 40.2 Kbps using GPRS). Do note that data rates are dependent on service providers.

For more information on the two cards, point your browser at *http://www. nokia.com/cda10/0,1119,2004,00.html.*

4. Give your profile a name, e.g., Home Network (see Figure 8-9). Also check the connection type(s) to be used for this profile. In other words, you can use this profile to connect to a WLAN connection, GSM connection, or GPRS connection (for our example here, let's just turn on the WLAN connection checkbox). Click Next.

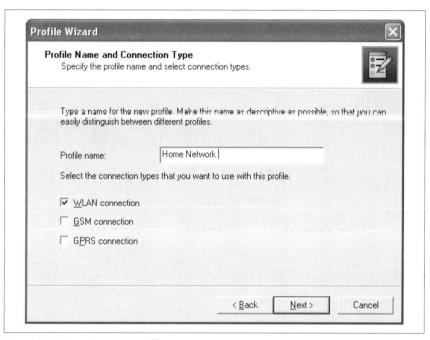

Figure 8-9. Creating a new profile

5. You will be prompted to select the wireless mode (Infrastructure or adhoc). The SSID(s) of the available wireless networks will also be displayed (see Figure 8-10). Select the SSID of the wireless network to which you want to connect. Click Next.

6. On the next screen, you have the option to specify your IP address manually. We will use the IP address allocated by the wireless network. Click Next.

7. The main screen of the Nokia D211 Manager will be displayed again (see Figure 8-8). Click Select... to choose the profile to use. Select the WLAN connection type under the Home Network item (see Figure 8-11).

8. You should now be able to connect to the wireless network. Information about the connection, such as the connection quality and data flow, is displayed (see Figure 8-12).

Configuring GPRS access. Let's now configure the Nokia D211 for GPRS access. For this, you need to insert your SIM card into the D211 before you can connect to the GPRS network. If you purchased the D211 or D311 along with a wireless plan from a cellular provider, the SIM card may have been installed for you. Otherwise, you will have to use a SIM card from another phone.

1. In the D211 Manager, click on Profiles, then click the Modify tab.
2. Select the profile to which you want to add GPRS access.
3. Click on GPRS (see Figure 8-13). Turn on the "Use GPRS connection with this profile" and "Specify access point name manually" options. Enter the GPRS access point name provided by your ISP.
4. Click OK and return to the main screen by clicking on the General tab.
5. Click Select... and choose the GPRS item (see Figure 8-14).
6. Click the Activate button (see Figure 8-15).
7. A Dial-up Connection window appears (see Figure 8-16). Enter your username and password (provided by your ISP).
8. When authenticated, you should now see the operational information (see Figure 8-17).

Messaging using SMS on the Nokia D211. One interesting feature of the Nokia D211 is the ability to send and receive SMS (Short Message Service) messages. In the Nokia D211 Manager window (see Figure 8-18), click SMS → Inbox (or any other items within the SMS menu to launch the Nokia Short Messaging window).

This window contains five main tabs: Inbox, Outbox, Sent messages, Delivery reports and Contacts (see Figure 8-19). To send a message, simply click the Send message icon and type your text.

CDMA2000

Besides GSM, Code Division Multiple Access (CDMA) is also a popular cellular technology used in the U.S. CDMA uses Spread Spectrum Technology (SST), which allows a unique code to be attached to each conversation and to spread conversations across wide segments of the cellular broadcast spectrum. Each receiver decodes on the same frequency segment as the sender. Because multiple signals can be transmitted over the same spectrum, CDMA allows many more conversations to be possible compared to other cellular technologies.

SMS Craze in Asia

SMS messaging is very popular in Asia. In Singapore, teenagers can often input text faster (using numeric keypads on the phones) than you can type on a computer keyboard!

The following is an explanation of how to type messages on your mobile phone.

Each numeric key on your phone is assigned three to four alphabetic characters:

```
2 - a, b, c
3 - d, e, f
4 - g, h, i
5 - j, k, l
6 - m, n, o
7 - p, q, r, s
8 - t, u, v
9 - w, x, y, z
```

To form a word, you need to press the corresponding digits that make up the letters of a word. For example, to form the word "is," you would press "4" three times ("i" is the third alphabet in this assignment) and then press "7" four times. This input method is commonly known as the "multitap" method.

But most mobile phones sold today support the T9 input method. T9 stands for "Text on 9 keys." Here is how T9 works. Look for the letters that you want and press the assigned digit once. Using the same example, to form the word "is," press "4," followed by "7." A phone utilizing the T9 technology has a compressed database of all the commonly used words. In this case, the database returns "is" as a likely word.

There are many cases when a particular key sequence may generate multiple words, such as the sequence "4663." Two possible words are "good" and "home." So, as a user you just need to select the word that you want. If a desired word cannot be found in the database, you have the option to add it in.

Try it on your mobile phone and see if you can type faster than on a keyboard!

For more information on T9 input, go to *http://www.t9.com/*.

TDMA

The predecessor of CDMA is Time Division Multiple Access (TDMA). TDMA operates similarly to network packet switching—it divides the signal into multiple segments, thereby allowing multiple calls to take place. Unlike CDMA, TDMA does not utilize Spread Spectrum Technology and hence the available spectrum must be divided into channels, which means fewer users are supported simultaneously than with CDMA.

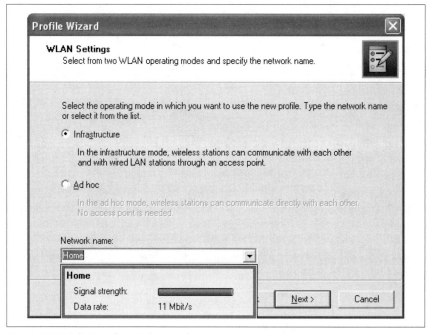

Figure 8-10. Selecting the wireless mode

CDMA is used by Sprint PCS, Verizon Wireless, and AT&T. CDMA2000 is the latest generation of CDMA technology and is used on Sprint's PCS Vision network and Verizon Wireless's Express Network.

Using the AirPrime PC3200 CDMA2000 PC Card

Sprint's AirPrime PC3200 PCMCIA card operates on the CDMA2000 network. This card dances on the edge of 2.5G and 3G, boasting typical data speeds of between 50 and 70 Kbps. It is capable of a peak speed of 144 Kbps.

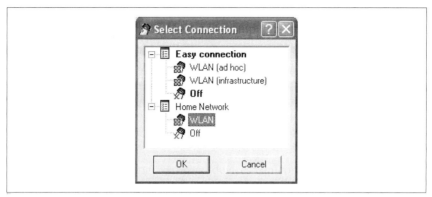

Figure 8-11. Selecting the wireless connection

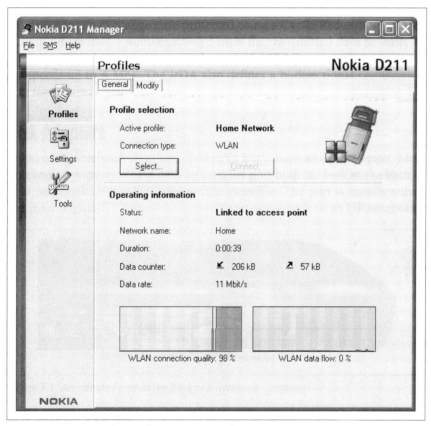

Figure 8-12. Viewing the wireless connection information

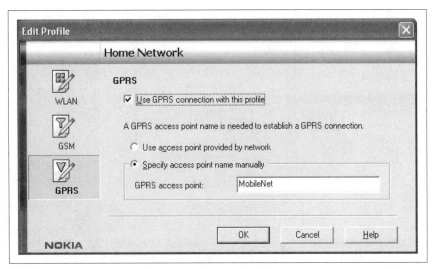

Figure 8-13. Using a GPRS connection

Figure 8-14. Selecting the GPRS connection

Figure 8-15. Activating GPRS access

Installing the AirPrime PC3200. Take the following steps to install the Air-Prime PC3200:

1. Install the provided software using the installation CD.

2. Insert the card into a PCMCIA slot on your notebook.

Figure 8-16. Dialing up GPRS

3. Windows XP will search for the appropriate drivers using wizards. Select the option "Install the software automatically", and then select Continue Anyway to continue with the installation.

4. When the software installation is complete, you need to activate the card (see the following section).

Activating the AirPrime PC3200. Before you can use the card, you need to activate it, which connects your account to the card and allows it to get on the Sprint PCS Vision network. Unlike with GSM/GPRS adapters and phones, CDMA does not use a SIM card, so your identity is connected with the account information you supply during this procedure.

After the software installation is complete, the Activation Wizard appears and provides you with the following sequence:

1. The first screen (Figure 8-20) provides you with basic information about the activation sequence. If you don't already have an activation code and phone number, follow the instructions on this screen to obtain them.

2. In the following screens, supply your activation code, phone number, and MSID (this may be the same as the phone number). When this sequence is complete, the final screen of the Activation Wizard appears (Figure 8-21).

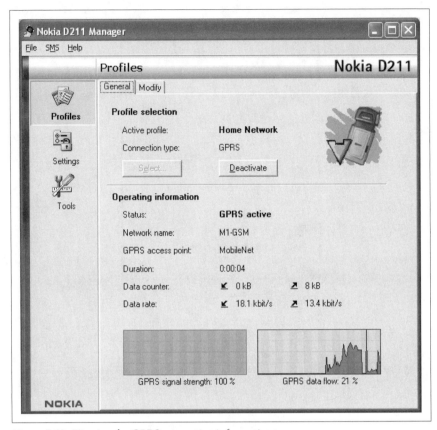

Figure 8-17. Viewing the GPRS connection information

Figure 8-18. Invoking the SMS functionality

3. After the Activation Wizard is complete, the PCS Connection Manager appears and begins the process of provisioning (Figure 8-22), which supplies your adapter with a valid IP address and whatever credentials are necessary to make future connections to the network. This is a one-time operation, and may take 15 minutes or more.

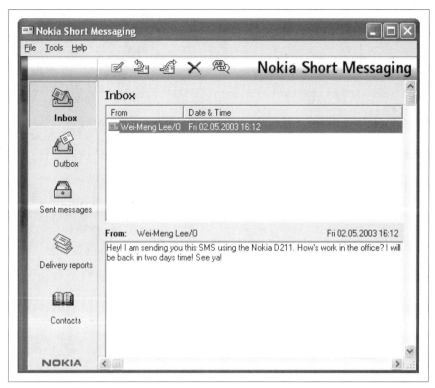

Figure 8-19. The Nokia Short Messaging window

Making the connection. After you've activated the card and gone through the provisioning process, the PCS Connection Manager will prompt you to "Click 'GO' to connect...". (If you get an error message, contact Sprint technical support.) To connect to the network, take the steps described next.

1. Click GO in the PCS Connection Manager window.

2. After the connection is made, you will see a splash screen, which you can disable in future sessions by deselecting "Show welcome screen".

3. Dismiss the splash screen by clicking OK, and you will return to the PCS Connection Manager, which now shows some basic network statistics (Figure 8-23).

4. Click Stop to disconnect from the network (you can now unplug the card until you need to use it again).

Each time you log in, the PCS Connection Manager is started automatically. You can close the window and minimize it to the system tray by clicking the "x" in the lower-right corner. Click the tray icon (see Figure 8-24) to restore the PCS Connection Manager window.

Tips for Road Warriors

Here are some tips for road warriors:

Use a wireless network whenever one is around. When you are traveling, such as on a train, you can manually switch to GPRS access. The downside is that GPRS access is slower and much more costly than wireless access. The theoretical speed of 40.2 Kbps is not achievable in practice. Expect performance of about 20+ Kbps.

Since GPRS is much slower and costs more, turn off image loading in your web browser when surfing the Web. This causes the web pages to load faster and save you money.

If your cellular provider supports a compressing proxy (See "Compression," later in this chapter), be sure to install and configure the software according to the instructions. Such a proxy server can increase speed and reduce your bandwidth consumption.

Speed for checking emails is acceptable when using GPRS. However, it is advisable to configure your email client to download message headers only; if someone sends you a multi-megabyte attachment or even a long message, it could take a long time to download and use up your bandwidth allotment. You can then decide on a message-by-message basis whether to view the message body and/or download attachments. You should also install a spam filter in your email application so as to avoid downloading huge junk emails just to delete them. Many email clients include some spam-blocking features, and typically analyze the email headers (rather than the body of the message) to determine whether a message is spam.

Make full use of the SMS feature. Sending SMS messages may be cheaper than making a voice call. Use SMS instead of voice calls: you can type them with the keyboard on your notebook and they will be delivered quickly.

The PCS Connection Manager displays precious little information. To see extended information, such as signal strength, click MENU and select Device Info & Diagnostics. (This option is only available while you are disconnected from the network; see Figure 8-25.)

Using the AirCard 555 CDMA2000 PC Card

Verizon offers the Sierra Wireless (*http://www.sierrawireless.com/*) AirCard 555 for notebook computer users of its Express Network service. As with the offerings from Sprint, you can expect between 50 and 70 Kbps with this card and Verizon's service, with a peak speed of144 Kbps.

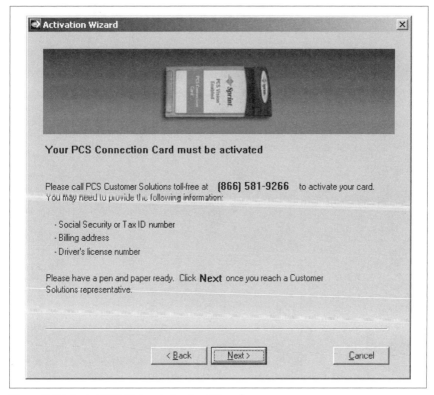

Figure 8-20. Sprint PCS Vision Activation Wizard

Installing the AirCard 555. Follow these steps to install the AirCard 555:

1. Install the provided software using the installation CD.

2. Insert the card into a PCMCIA slot on your notebook.

3. Windows XP will search for the appropriate drivers using wizards. Select the option "Install the software automatically", and then select Continue Anyway to continue with the installation.

4. When the software installation is complete, you need to activate the card (see the following section).

Making the connection. After you've installed the software, insert the Air-Card into your PCMCIA slot. Windows XP detects the card and installs the drivers (you may need to click through some confirmation dialogs). When that is finished, your system tray will indicate that a new network device has been detected (see Figure 8-26). You can ignore this.

After a few seconds, things settle down, and the AirCard 555 Watcher icon appears in the tray (the left-most icon shown in Figure 8-27). This icon is

Figure 8-21. The final step of the Activation Wizard

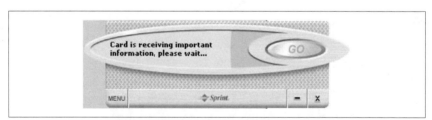

Figure 8-22. The PCS Connection Manager during provisioning

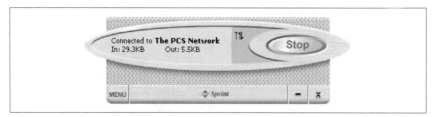

Figure 8-23. PCS Connection Manager showing network usage statistics

Figure 8-24. PCS Connection Manager system tray icon

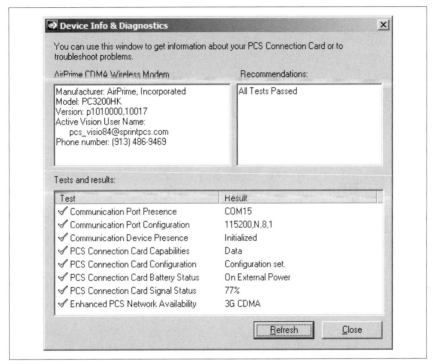

Figure 8-25. Device Info & Diagnostics showing device information and network signal status

only available when the AirCard is plugged into your computer. Click it to bring the Watcher window to the front (Figure 8-28).

The AirCard 555 Watcher (Figure 8-28) shows the signal strength (one out of five bars in this figure). To connect to the network, click Connect. Within a few seconds, you should be able to access the Internet. You can also send and receive SMSs using the Watcher. Click Tools → Mobile Messenger to access this feature (you do not need to be connected to send or receive an SMS, but you must be in the service area).

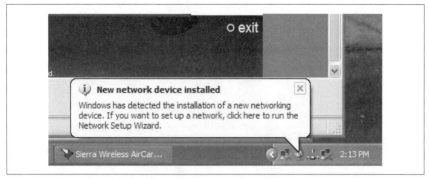

Figure 8-26. Windows XP detecting the AirCard

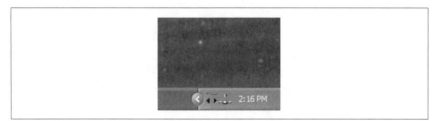

Figure 8-27. The AirCard 555 Watcher icon appearing in the system tray

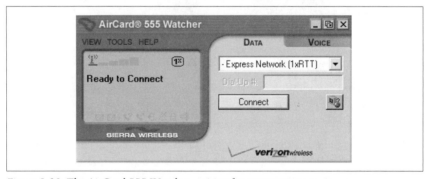

Figure 8-28. The AirCard 555 Watcher waiting for you to connect

Compression

Although GPRS and CDMA2000 can reach speeds faster than a regular dial-up Internet connection, they can't compete with a good solid Wi-Fi connection. But, they can get slightly closer by putting a little intelligence between your notebook and the Internet.

Verizon and AT&T Wireless support a *compressing proxy server*. This involves two pieces of middleware that sit between your web browser and the Internet, which are described next.

The compressing proxy server

This is a proxy server that sits in your cellular carrier's "cloud" (somewhere on their network). When a request comes in for a web document, such as an HTML file, graphic, or text file, this proxy server downloads the content, compresses it, and sends it back to whoever requested it (you).

The client

Because your web browser doesn't understand the compression scheme used by the proxy server up in the cloud, there is a second piece of software that runs on your computer. This is often referred to as a client and is generally invisible to you. This client is actually a mini proxy server that accepts requests from your web browser, forwards them to the compressing server in the cloud, and decompresses the responses before sending them back to your browser.

The upshot of this arrangement is that you can expect load times to be significantly reduced in many circumstances. For example, under poor network connections (with the signal meter reading one out of five bars), Verizon's compressing proxy was able to transfer an 814-kilobyte text file in 98 seconds—a speed of 8.3K per second. Compare this to a transfer under the same network conditions but without the compressing proxy, which took 15 minutes and 5 seconds!

The compressing proxies can also compress images. Figures 8-29, 8-30, and 8-31 show detail from an image that was compressed using three different compression settings (lowest quality, highest compression, 6155 bytes; medium quality, medium compression, 10419 bytes; and no compression at all, 16918 bytes).

In Figure 8-30, artifacts are barely visible; even though the file size is roughly 60 percent of the uncompressed version, it is hard to tell the difference between the two.

You should ask your wireless carrier about this capability because they may not call attention to it when you subscribe for service. At the time of this writing, the following offerings are available from major providers in the United States:

AT&T Wireless

AT&T provides an Optimization Manager as part of their Communication Manager. To download the Communication Manager, visit *http://support.attws.com*, and click the link for downloads.

Figure 8-29. Photograph showing maximum compression

Figure 8-30. Photograph showing a medium level compression

Verizon Wireless

Verizon includes Venturi (*http://www.venturiwireless.com/*) compression software with the Sierra Wireless AirCard 555.

T-Mobile

T-Mobile uses a service called T-Mobile Internet Accelerator. Unlike the solutions described in this section, this is completely clientless; it transparently intercepts and compresses network traffic so that images and documents that your web browser receives are as small as possible.

Figure 8-31. Photograph showing no compression

Sprint

As with T-Mobile, Sprint's PCS Vision network uses transparent compression built into their network infrastructure. Sprint's compression capabilities are provided by Bytemobile (*http://www.bytemobile.com/*).

CHAPTER NINE

Global Positioning System (GPS)

Have you ever lost your way when you were in a foreign country, state, or even your neighborhood? You could use a map to help orient yourself. But if you are in a foreign land, this is not always an easy task.

This is where the Global Positioning System (GPS) comes in. Using GPS, you can find out precisely where you are on earth, and, when equipped with the appropriate mapping software, you can get driving instructions to bring you to your destination.

In this chapter, I explain how GPS works and how you can equip your Windows XP notebook with a GPS receiver and mapping software. We will go driving with our GPS and even have a little Wi-Fi fun!!

How GPS Works

The Global Positioning System consists of 27 earth-orbiting satellites (of which 24 are operational and 3 are backups) circling the earth twice each day. These satellites are arranged in six orbital paths, as shown in Figure 9-1.

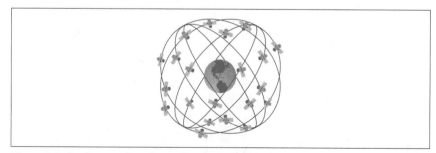

Figure 9-1. Satellites circling the earth in six orbital paths

These satellites continuously emit coded *positional* and *timing* information using low-power radio waves at frequencies in the 1500 MHz range. GPS receivers on earth then pick up the signals and calculate the exact* positioning on earth. The orbits of the satellites are arranged in such a manner that at any one time, four satellites are visible. Thus, a GPS receiver is able to receive signals from these four satellites and, based on the various signals transmitted by them, derive positional information on earth.

So how does the GPS receiver calculate its position? It does so by measuring the distance between itself and the satellites. Signals emitted by the satellites will be received by the GPS receiver after a time lag, and based on the speed of light, the GPS receiver can calculate the distance from itself to the satellite. But getting the distance away from one satellite is not enough, since it tells you only that you are anywhere on the surface of the sphere (think in terms of three-dimensional space). Figure 9-2 shows that you can be anywhere on the sphere surrounding the satellite.

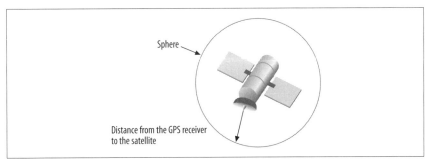

Figure 9-2. A sphere containing all the possible positions

To pinpoint your exact location, GPS uses a technique call *triangulation*. It uses at least three satellites to pinpoint an exact location on earth. Figure 9-3 shows that if you have two satellites, then you can narrow down your location to the intersection of the two spheres. In this case, you can be anywhere on the dotted line (which is a circle).

This is not precise enough. With a third satellite, you can reduce the possibilities to two (see Figure 9-4). But one of these two points is in space, which is not likely the position you are in. Hence you can effectively derive your position from three satellites.

---

* Exact positioning is dependent on many factors, such as the type of receiver used and whether Selective Availability (see the sidebar "Accuracy of GPS," later in this chapter, for more information) is turned on. In general, the precision of positioning can be anywhere from 5 meters to 100 meters.

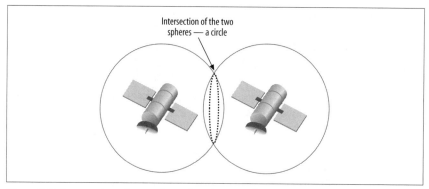

Figure 9-3. Intersection of two spheres forming a circle

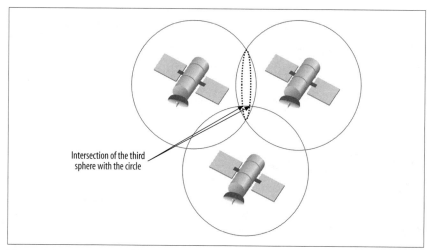

Figure 9-4. Intersections of the circle (formed by the two intersecting spheres) with a third sphere

Most GPS receivers use information from three or more satellites to increase the accuracy of the positional information.

Uses of GPS

The function of GPS is fairly straightforward—with a GPS receiver, you can obtain your positional information in the form of longitude, latitude, and altitude. What is important is the way you use this information. Some useful applications of GPS are described next.

Accuracy of GPS

GPS was originally developed in the 1980s by the U.S. Department of Defense for military use. Because it was designed primarily for the military, the U.S. Department of Defense introduced Selective Availability (SA) to degrade the signal accuracy and to encrypt sensitive information, so that civilian usage could be restricted. The satellites would deliberately broadcast wrong and randomly inaccurate signals, which would cause the precision of the GPS data to be within 100 meters. The accurate information could only be decoded by the military.

Because of the great commercial potential of GPS, in May 2000, President Clinton announced that the U.S would no longer degrade the accuracy of GPS. With SA turned off, the accuracy of the GPS data could be within 3 meters.

In the second Gulf war against Iraq in 2003, the United States reportedly degraded the GPS system so that Iraq could not make use of GPS against U.S. forces. While this is good news for the military, it certainly affected all those who rely on GPS for their daily activities. So, if you arrived at the wrong destination using a GPS navigational system, now you know why!

Military use

As GPS was originally developed for military use, the U.S. Department of Defense is the main user of the technology. The use of GPS for guiding "smart" bombs has played an important role in recent wars, especially in the Persian Gulf.

Location Based Services (LBS)

GPS has been increasingly deployed in the commercial scene. Location Based Services make use of the knowledge of your precise location to provide location-sensitive services. For example, you can use location-based services to give you a list of restaurants near your current location.

Navigation services

GPS is popularly used for navigational purposes, such as driving and flying. A GPS-enabled PDA can help a driver to navigate unfamiliar cities. GPS is also widely used in the shipping industry as well as in airplane navigational systems. Courier companies such as UPS and FedEx make extensive use of GPS in their delivery infrastructures.

Tracking

Using GPS to track the whereabouts of people or objects is rapidly gaining acceptance. This is useful in the medical sector where patients suffering from diseases such as Alzheimer's can wear a GPS watch, and when needed, press a panic button to reveal their exact location to their family members.

Mapping

GPS is also popularly used in mapping software, allowing you to combine a GPS receiver with mapping software to display your current location. This is useful for travelers or explorers who need navigational aids.

A GPS Glossary

Here are some GPS terms that you will encounter when you use GPS and GPS software:

Waypoint

A location that you store in your GPS system (as coordinates). Examples of waypoints are a hiking location, camping ground, church, or any places of interest to a GPS user. You normally add a waypoint to your GPS before you start your traveling. You can also add one during your travel when you locate a place of interest.

Route

A collection of waypoints representing the path that you would like to take.

Latitude, Longitude, and Altitude

The coordinates of a specific location on earth. These three pieces of information together define a point in the three-dimensional space.

Bearing

The direction you are aiming for.

Heading

The actual direction you are traveling towards. It is not the same as bearing. Bearing is your desired direction, but you may not be heading towards the desired direction due to factors such as obstacles (e.g., water, fences, and mountains). Therefore, you have to momentarily head in another direction in a bid to get to your destination.

Fix

A location returned by the GPS receiver after processing the readings of at least three satellites.

TTFF (Time to First Fix)

The least amount of time required to get a fix by the minimum number of satellites required for triangulation. Normally it takes a few minutes before you can get a fix.

NMEA (National Marine Electronics Association)

The NMEA-0183 standard has been universally adopted by GPS manufacturers and virtually every GPS product for exchanging navigational information between devices. NMEA-0183 defines a "sentence" format (using printable ASCII text) describing navigational information.

8/12 channels receiver

An 8-channel receiver uses 8 channels to access 8 different satellites at any one time. A 12-channel receiver can access 12 satellites at once.

Selective Availability (SA)

The degrading of GPS signals and the encryption of GPS data for nonmilitary use. See the sidebar "Accuracy of GPS" earlier in this chapter for more information on SA.

CEP, RMS, and 2D RMS

Circular Error Probable (CEP), RMS (Root Mean Square), and 2D RMS are all measures of the accuracy of a GPS receiver. CEP represents the radius of a circle containing 50 percent of the GPS readings. RMS represents the radius of a circle containing 68 percent of the GPS readings. 2D RMS represents the radius of a circle containing 98 percent of the GPS readings. If 3 GPS receivers each claims to have 2m CEP, 2m RMS and 2m 2D RMS respectively, then the third one is the most accurate, since it has readings accurate to within a 2-meter radius 98 percent of the time.

GPS Devices

There are two main types of GPS receivers available in the market at the moment:

- Plain GPS receivers
- GPS receivers with maps

A plain GPS receiver simply interprets the readings from the satellite and returns the result in latitude, longitude, and altitude. Figure 9-5 shows the PocketMap (*http://www.pocketmap.com*) PMG-220 CF GPS receiver. You can use the PMG-220 on your Pocket PC or your Windows XP notebook (which requires a PCMCIA sleeve for the CF card). Plain GPS receivers are useful in cases where you want to use the receiver interchangeably on your Pocket PC or Windows XP notebook computer. You also have the flexibility to use them with any other mapping software.

Figure 9-6 shows the Emtac Bluetooth GPS receiver. The nice feature of this receiver is that it does not occupy a Compact Flash slot on your Pocket PC for GPS functionality. You can connect to it wirelessly using Bluetooth and position it at a location where you can get a good signal.

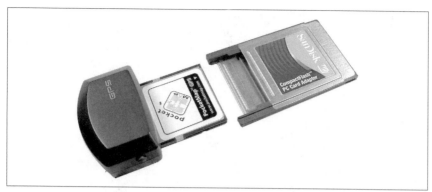

*Figure 9-5. The PocketMap PMG-220 Compact Flash GPS receiver
with a CompactFlash to PCMCIA sleeve*

Figure 9-6. The Emtac Bluetooth GPS receiver

Figure 9-7 shows two standalone GPS receivers equipped with their own mapping software. The Magellan Meridian Gold and the Garmin StreetPilot III contain built-in screens to display maps. There is no need to connect the receivers to any device for them to work. Standalone GPS receivers are useful for travelers who need a lightweight GPS solution.

Installing a GPS

There's generally not much to installing a GPS device. To Windows XP, most GPS devices look like a COM port (also known as a serial port, best

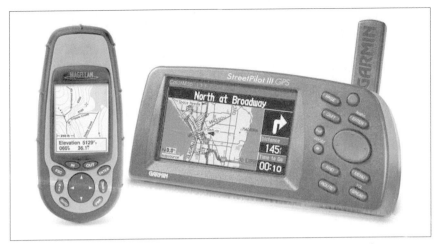

Figure 9-7. The Magellan Meridian Gold GPS (left) and the Garmin StreetPilot III (Magellen used by permission, Thales Navigation, Inc. 2003; Garmin courtesy of Garmin Ltd.)

known for connecting modems to your computer). Most consumer GPS devices use serial port settings of 4800,N,8,1, which is serial port shorthand for the underwhelming speed of 4800 bps, no parity, 8 data bits, and 1 stop bit. The GPS spews information to that COM port.

If you're interested in seeing what the GPS has to say, do the following:

1. Launch HyperTerminal (Start → All Programs → Accessories → Communications → HyperTerminal).

2. When prompted, supply a description for the connection (such as GPS, as shown in Figure 9-8). Click OK. This brings up the Connect To dialog.

3. Next, select the COM port that your GPS uses (see the documentation that came with your GPS for this information), as shown in Figure 9-9. Click OK. This brings up the COM port Properties dialog.

4. Set the properties to 4800, 8, None, 1, and None, as shown in Figure 9-10. Click OK.

If all went well, you should start seeing all kinds of nonsense appear on your screen, as shown in Figure 9-11.

GPS Software

A GPS receiver receives coordinate information about its location and that's it. To put the location information to good use, you need mapping software

Figure 9-8. Creating a new connection with HyperTerminal

Figure 9-9. Connecting to the GPS COM port

that is able to take in the location information and return something, per-haps a map showing you where you are. Some mapping software goes the extra mile in helping you to navigate routes based on the end point that you have defined.

Here is a list mapping software that is worth exploring:

- Microsoft Streets and Trips (*http://www.microsoft.com/streets/*)
- MapPoint (*http://www.microsoft.com/mappoint/*)

Figure 9-10. Setting COM port properties in HyperTerminal

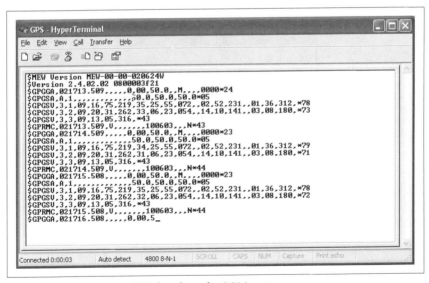

Figure 9-11. Viewing raw GPS data from the COM port

- MapPoint Web Service (*http://www.microsoft.com/mappoint/net/*)
- EarthViewer3D (*http://www.earthviewer.com*)
- GPS3D (*http://www.mgix.com/gps3d/*)
- VisualGPS (*http://www.visualgps.net/VisualGPS/*)
- GPS Trackmaker (*http://www.gpstm.com/*)
- USAPhotoMaps (*http://jdmcox.com/*)

In the next section, I show you how you can use the Microsoft Streets and Trips together with your GPS receiver to display a map showing your current location.

Microsoft Streets and Trips

Microsoft Streets and Trips is an affordable (less than $40) mapping package based on MapPoint technology. It has comprehensive maps of the U.S. and Canada, and lets you locate addresses, plan routes, and export maps to a Pocket PC. It also can use a GPS receiver to keep track of your location at all times.

To configure Streets and Trips to use a GPS:

1. Select Tools → GPS → Configure GPS Receiver. The GPS Receiver settings dialog appears (Figure 9-12).

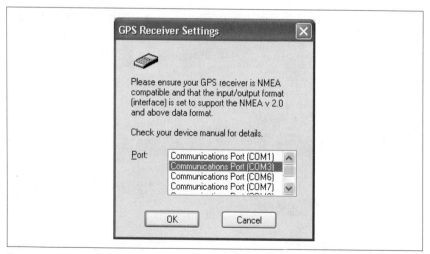

Figure 9-12. Configuring Microsoft Streets and Trips for a GPS receiver

2. Select the COM port your GPS is installed on and click OK.

3. Next, select Tools → GPS → Track Position. The GPS Sensor window appears (Figure 9-13). (If you close this window, you can bring it back up with Tools → GPS → GPS Sensor.)

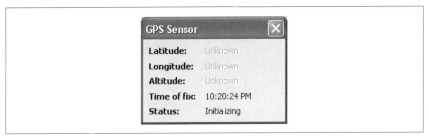

Figure 9-13. Microsoft Streets and Trips waiting for data from the GPS receiver

After some time (a few seconds to several minutes), Streets and Trips will begin getting positional data from the GPS, and it will show your location as you can see in Figure 9-14.

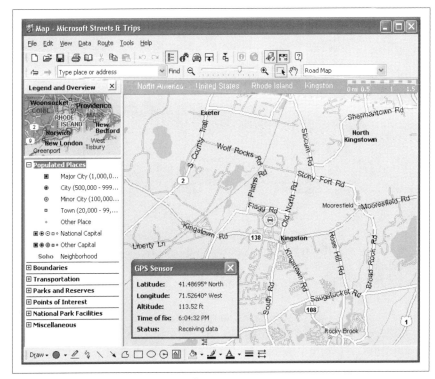

Figure 9-14. Pinpointing a location with GPS

NetStumbler and GPS

Chapter 3 introduced NetStumbler (*http://www.netstumbler.com*), a free application for discovering wireless networks. If you attach a compatible GPS to your computer, you can configure NetStumbler to read data from the GPS. Then, you can drive around while it's scanning and generate maps of wireless access points.

To configure NetStumbler for GPS, make sure that it is installed and working, and that you've installed your GPS device according to the GPS vendor's instructions. You'll need to know the COM port that your GPS uses (see your GPS documentation). To get NetStumbler to read data from the GPS, follow these steps:

1. In NetStumbler, select View → Options. This brings up the Network Stumbler Options dialog.

2. Click the GPS tab (Figure 9-15). Set the protocol, COM port, and communications settings to match your GPS device. Click OK.

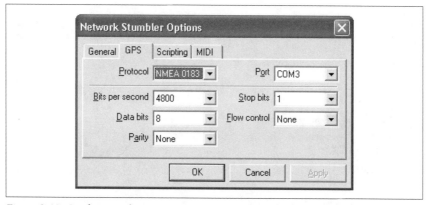

Figure 9-15. Configuring the communication settings to match your GPS device

3. Examine the lower-right corner of the NetStumbler window. You will probably see the message "No position fix" for anywhere from a few seconds to 15 minutes. After a while, it should be replaced by your longitude and latitude. If it does not display this information, your GPS may not be able to get a fix. Orient the antenna so that it has a clear view of the sky, and run any diagnostic software that came with your GPS or a free utility such as VisualGPS (exit NetStumbler first, since only one program can access the GPS at a time) to see if you can get a signal.

You can also configure NetStumbler's scan speed (click the General tab in Network Stumbler Options; see Figure 9-16). Fast will scan every 0.5 seconds and slow will scan every 1.5 seconds. If you select "Auto Adjust using GPS", NetStumbler will adjust its scan rate based on how fast you are traveling.

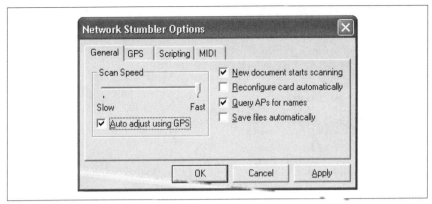

Figure 9-16. Setting the NetStumbler scan speed

COM port hell. At the time of this writing, NetStumbler supports COM ports between 1 and 8. If your GPS was assigned a higher COM port, you can adjust serial port allocations as follows:

1. Bring up the Device Manager (right-click My Computer, choose Properties, then choose Hardware → Device Manager).

2. Expand the node marked Ports (COM & LPT) and examine the current COM port assignments (see Figure 9-17). You will need to find the one that corresponds to your GPS device.

3. Double-click the port you want to change. This brings up the Properties dialog.

4. Click Port Settings → Advanced. This brings up the Advanced Settings dialog (see Figure 9-18). Set the COM Port Number to the desired setting (If the port is marked as In Use, you must free that port; check the settings of other ports, as well as modems in the device manager to see if you can reassign them.)

> One common source of in-use ports is Bluetooth. Use the Bluetooth setup (right-click the Bluetooth icon in the system tray and click Setup → Configuration) to alter the port settings. Better yet, install your Bluetooth drivers after you've installed your GPS. (If you're so inclined, you can uninstall both the GPS and Bluetooth drivers and repeat the installation.)

Safety. If you plan to do some Wardriving (see Chapter 3) with NetStumbler, keep the following in mind:

- Put the computer somewhere safe and out of the way. Don't put it someplace where a sudden stop will send it into your lap or through a window.

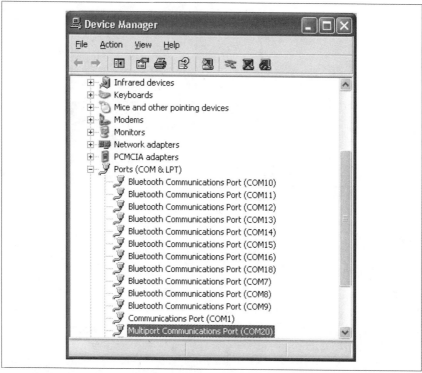

Figure 9-17. Viewing COM port assignments in the Device Manager

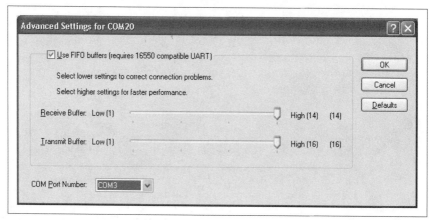

Figure 9-18. Reassigning COM20 to COM3

- Forget that the computer is there while you are driving. If you have to fiddle with it, pull over first. If you can have a friend driving with you who can operate the computer, all the better. Do not let the computer distract you while you are driving.

- Make sure that the GPS gets a fix before you start driving. It's a lot harder for it to get a fix while you are in motion.

- Put the GPS somewhere where it can easily pick up the satellite signals. Your best bet is to get a magnetized external antenna that can attach to your roof. Be sure that there are no loose wires sticking out of your window. Don't slam the wires in the door!

 When you are driving a car, your first responsibility is to drive safely. Pay attention to the road and drive carefully.

Generating maps. After you've finished doing a scan with NetStumbler, you should be sure to save the file (File → Save) so that you can access it later or generate maps with it. WiFiMaps.com (*http://wifimaps.com/*) lets you upload scan files, then it stores the information, making detailed maps of Wi-Fi access points to anyone who visits their site. (If this prospect troubles you, you can check their site to see if your access point is listed; their FAQ includes instructions for having your access point removed from their database.)

This book's editor, Brian Jepson, got so excited about this that he wrote a simple web application to generate a map using the summary format that NetStumbler exports (File → Export → Summary). This program uses the 1990 U.S. Census map server (*http://tiger.census.gov/cgi-bin/mapsurfer*). To generate your own maps, all you need to do is visit *http://www.jepstone.net/stumbler* with a web browser, use the web page to upload your NetStumbler summary file, and wait for it to render the map. Figure 9-19 shows a sample map from southern Rhode Island.

This program does not store the maps for very long—just a couple of days so you can revisit the map a few times if you'd like—and does not publish the information you upload publicly. It's just there for one-offs.

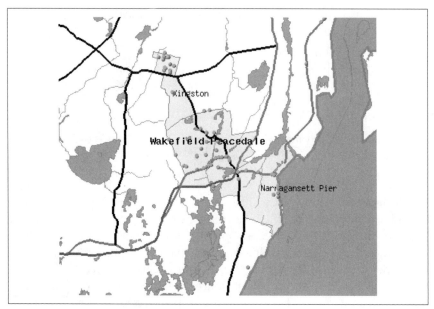

Figure 9-19. Mapping access points in southern Rhode Island

CHAPTER TEN

Microsoft Smart Display
and Remote Desktop

Many people have cordless phones at home and in the office. Instead of using a tethered phone, a cordless phone allows you the freedom to use the phone anywhere in the house, without the constraints of wires. The same concept applies to computing. How often have you dreamed of using your computers anywhere in your home? A notebook computer is one such solution. However, if your primary computer is a desktop system, synchronizing documents created or modified on the notebook with your desktop is always a chore. It would be better to use the same desktop computer but with the mobility to use it anywhere at home—in the garden, garage, or even the washroom!

Microsoft thought of this concept and calls it the *Microsoft Smart Display* (previously code-named "Mira"). In this chapter, I explain what a Smart Display is and how you can use it together with your Windows XP computer. I also explain Remote Desktop, the underlying service behind the Smart Display, and how you can use it to connect from one computer to another.

What Is the Microsoft Smart Display?

Microsoft defines the Smart Display as a wireless touch-screen monitor that allow you to access your computer from anywhere in your home. Think of it as just your conventional LCD monitor, but with Wi-Fi built in and the ability to write on the screen directly.

On the technical side, a Smart Display uses the Windows CE for Smart Display operating system, a version based on Windows CE .NET 4.1. On the host computer, you need Windows XP Professional Edition (Service Pack 1). This is because the Smart Display makes use of Remote Desktop for displaying the output remotely, which is available in the Windows XP Professional edition but not in the Home edition. This is shown in Figure 10-1.

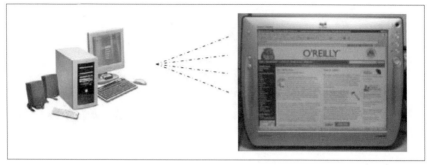

Figure 10-1. How Smart Display works

When you use the Smart Display to connect to the host computer, the host computer will be not be usable; only one user is allowed to use the computer at any one time. This is a limitation that Microsoft says it will resolve in the next version of the Smart Display.

Using the ViewSonic AirPanel V150

The ViewSonic AirPanel V150 (see Figure 10-2) is a 15" Smart Display utilizing the Intel's XScale PX250 processor running at 400 MHz. It comes with 32 MB of ROM and 64 MB of SDRAM. Weighing a mere six pounds, it is quite easy to lug around the house. A fully charged battery allows the AirPanel to last for four hours (a decent duration—just remember to charge it every alternate night if you use it on a regular basis).

Figure 10-2. The ViewSonic AirPanel V150

The AirPanel screen can support a maximum resolution of 1024 by 768. With an optional docking station (see Figure 10-3), you can use the Air-Panel as your primary monitor.

Figure 10-3. The optional AirPanel dock

The AirPanel comes with the following features (see Figure 10-4):

- Directional pad with left and right button functionality
- Handwriting recognition
- On-screen keyboard
- Two USB ports and one PC card slot
- Microphone and speaker jacks

The AirPanel V150 also includes the 802.11b AirSync USB wireless adapter (see Figure 10-5). You need to connect this to your host computer so that the AirPanel can connect to it wirelessly (this is not needed if you already have a Wi-Fi adapter).

Connecting the AirPanel to Your Host Computer

There are a few ways to connect the AirPanel to your desktop:

- The simplest way is to use the included AirSync USB Wireless adapter. Connect the AirSync adapter and your AirPanel to your desktop using the included USB cable. Install the included setup application. Your

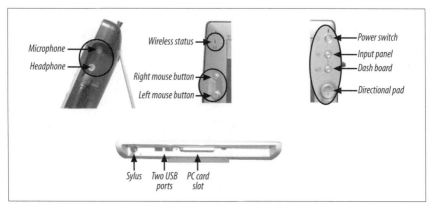

Figure 10-4. Expansion slots on the AirPanel V150

Figure 10-5. The AirSync USB Wireless adapter

available user accounts on the desktop will be copied to the AirPanel. This method is the most straightforward. It uses the wireless ad-hoc mode and does not require the use of access points.

- If you have an existing wireless card in your computer (common for notebook users), you can either use the included AirSync USB adapter or the existing wireless card to communicate with the AirPanel. However, if you use your existing wireless card to connect to the AirPanel, you will not be able to connect to your network (and Internet). The best option would be to use the AirSync for connecting to the AirPanel and to use your existing wireless card for Internet or network access. This approach still uses the ad-hoc mode for connecting to the AirPanel.

- If your desktop is connected to a wireless access point (through a wired connection), you need not use the AirSync for ad-hoc networking. You can connect the AirPanel through the access point. This mode uses the infrastructure mode.

Connecting via ad-hoc mode. By default, the Smart Display connects to your computer using ad-hoc mode. Using the installation CD, install the Microsoft Smart Display services by following the instructions on the screen.

Prior to this, you also need to connect your Smart Display to your computer using the provided USB cable. The Smart Display services will automatically copy the account(s) on your host computer to the Smart Display.

When you insert the supplied CD, the window in Figure 10-6 will be displayed. Select the desired language.

Figure 10-6. Installing the Smart Display services for the ViewSonic AirPanel

You will need to connect the AirSync USB Adapter to your computer (see Figure 10-7). You can also reuse your existing wireless adapter.

The accounts used to log in to your host computer must have a password, or else you will be prompted to supply a password for accounts that are used to log in to the host computer (see Figure 10-8).

If you have an existing wireless adapter, you can choose to use it (see Figure 10-9). Otherwise, you can leave it alone and use the provided AirSync to connect to the AirPanel.

If you have more than one wireless adapter, you will be prompted to select the adapter to configure for connecting to the AirPanel (see Figure 10-10).

Once the configuration is done, you will be shown the configuration information (Figure 10-11). I suggest you print out this window (press the Print button) so that you can use it to check on your AirPanel if you have a connection problem later on.

Figure 10-7. Connecting the AirSync wireless adapter

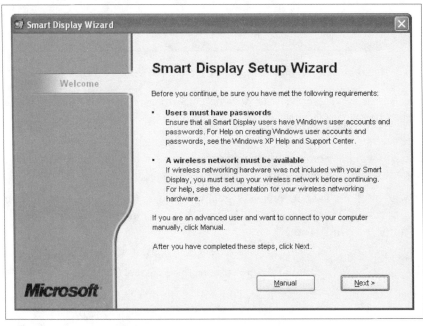

Figure 10-8. Requirements for using the AirPanel

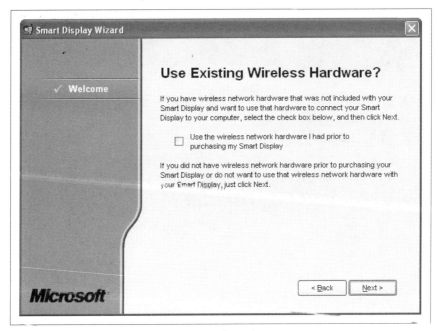

Figure 10-9. You can reuse your existing wireless adapter

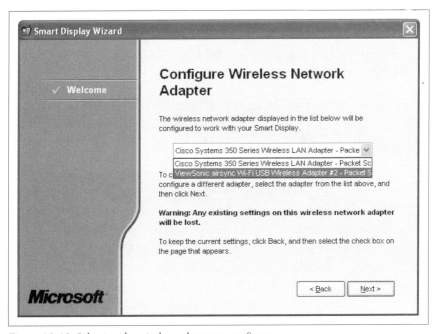

Figure 10-10. Selecting the wireless adapter to configure

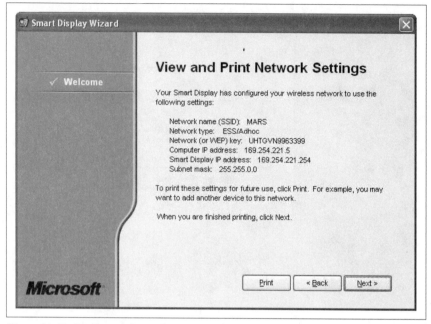

Figure 10-11. Displaying the configuration information

Finally, you will be prompted to select the account(s) that will be copied to the AirPanel (see Figure 10-12).

That's it! On the AirPanel, use the stylus to tap on the user account to log in to the host computer.

Connecting via infrastructure mode. Using infrastructure mode is straightforward: you just need to install the Microsoft Smart Display services on the target machine and configure your Smart Display to connect to it. There is no need to use the included AirSync wireless adapter. This configuration is suitable for office environments where your computer is connected to a network and you want to use the AirPanel in a meeting room with wireless access. On the AirPanel:

1. Click on the Settings icon and select the General tab.
2. Under the New connection group, click on the New... button.
3. Supply the username and computer name of the computer that you want to connect to (with the Microsoft Smart Display services installed).
4. You may optionally supply the password now so that when you connect to the computer in the future you will not need to supply the password again. But if you lose the AirPanel, your computer will not be secure anymore!

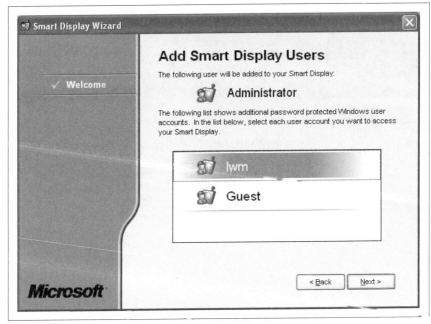

Figure 10-12. Copying the accounts to the AirPanel

5. Under the Advanced tab, ensure that you check the option to obtain an IP address using DHCP.

Some Tips for Connecting Your AirPanel V150

If you encounter problems in connecting your AirPanel to your computer, try the following:

- If you are accessing through an access point, ensure that you add the MAC address of your AirPanel to your access point (if you enable MAC address filtering, see "MAC Address Filtering" in Chapter 5). The MAC address of the AirPanel can be obtained via Settings → System Info (on the AirPanel itself).

- If your AirPanel connects to your desktop via ad-hoc mode, the AirPanel uses a fixed IP address. If you are using infrastructure mode, ensure that you use DHCP to obtain an IP address for the AirPanel. You can go to the Settings button on the AirPanel to configure the IP address.

- The best way to solve a connection problem would be to use the Connection Troubleshooter located in Programs → Microsoft Smart Display Services. Simply use the included USB cable to connect the AirPanel to your computer and click on "Scan your Smart Display connections" (see Figure 10-13).

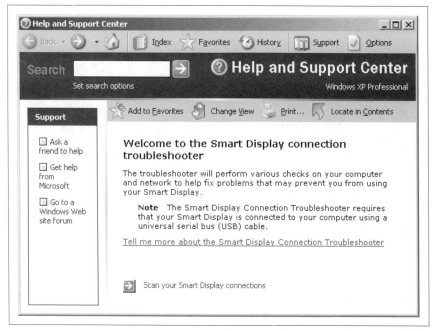

Figure 10-13. Using the Connection Troubleshooter to solve common connection problems

- Use the Connection Troubleshooter to see the WEP key generated (it is automatically generated by the Connection Troubleshooter). You need to enter this key into your AirPanel. WEP is used in ad-hoc mode when you use the Connection Troubleshooter to establish a connection between your computer and the AirPanel. If you are using infrastructure mode, WEP is optional.

Connecting Peripherals to the AirPanel

In most cases, the AirPanel is useful for tasks that do not require much input. Reading email and surfing the Web using the AirPanel is quite neat, considering that you can bring the monitor around the house and find a comfortable position to do so.

However, when it comes to input-intensive tasks such writing emails and using instant messaging, the shortcomings of the AirPanel become apparent. The onscreen keyboard is too slow and the handwriting recognition is not accurate enough. This is due to the touch screen technology used. The AirPanel is still using the older pressure-sensitive technology found in Pocket PCs, unlike the new Tablet PC's magnetic pen technology. And so, resting your hand on the screen would often cause you to click on items unintentionally. Writing on the screen is not natural and requires you to write legibly.

For typing, you can attach a USB keyboard to the AirPanel (see Figure 10-14). You can also attach a USB mouse to help in the navigation. One challenge in using the AirPanel for web surfing is that without using a mouse, it is difficult to identify hyperlinks—there is no mouse cursor to indicate when you are hovering over a hyperlink. If the AirPanel were to use the magnetic pen technology, then the hovering cursor would be visible to give visual cues.

Figure 10-14. Attaching a USB keyboard to the AirPanel

Using Remote Desktop

One of the tools shipped with Windows XP Professional is Remote Desktop. Remote Desktop allows you to connect to a remote computer (see Figure 10-15) as if you were sitting right in front of it. This is useful in situations where you need to access the network resource in your office while you are on the road (in which case Remote Desktop should be used through a VPN; see "Virtual Private Networks" in Chapter 4).

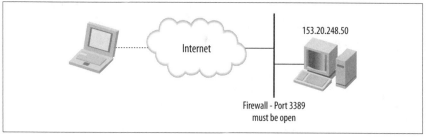

Figure 10-15. How Remote Desktop works

Remote Desktop uses the Remote Desktop Protocol (RDP), the same protocol used by Terminal Server (also known as Terminal Services in Windows 2000). Remote Desktop works on low-bandwidth connections, since it transmits only keystrokes and mouse events to the host, which then sends back screen information for the client to display.

> Remote Desktop is only available in Windows XP Professional. It is not included in Windows XP Home Edition.

Setting Up Remote Desktop

To allow remote users to connect to your computer:

1. Click Start → Settings → Control Panel → System and select the Remote tab (see Figure 10-16).

> If your machine is located behind a firewall, you need to open up port 3389. See "Opening a Port" in Chapter 5.

2. Turn on the "Allow users to connect remotely to this computer" checkbox.

3. By default, administrators are given access. Click on the Select Remote Users... button to give access rights to other nonadministrator users (see Figure 10-17).

Using Remote Desktop

To use Remote Desktop to connect to the remote host:

1. Go to Start → Programs → Accessories → Communications → Remote Desktop Connection (see Figure 10-18).

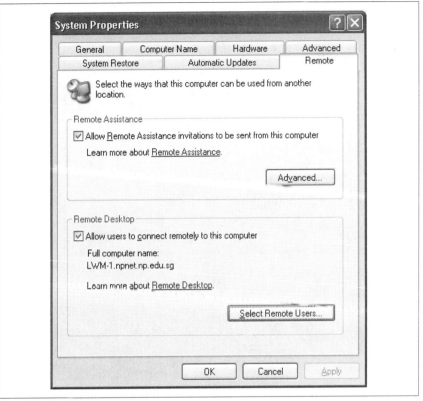

Figure 10-16. Allowing remote access to the computer

Remote Desktop Clients for Other Operating Systems

You can download Remote Desktop clients for operating systems other than Windows XP at the Microsoft web site, at *http://www.microsoft.com/ windowsxp/pro/downloads/rdclientdl.asp*.

This download installs the remote desktop client for Windows 95, Windows 98 Second Edition, Windows ME, Windows NT 4, or Windows 2000.

If you are using Mac OS X, you can download the Remote Desktop Client (RDC) from *http://www.microsoft.com/mac/DOWNLOAD/MISC/RDC.asp*. Figure 10-19 shows the RDC connected to Windows 2000 Advanced Server.

For Unix users, you can download rdesktop, an open source client for Windows NT Terminal Server and Windows 2000 Terminal Services, from *http:// www.rdesktop.org*.

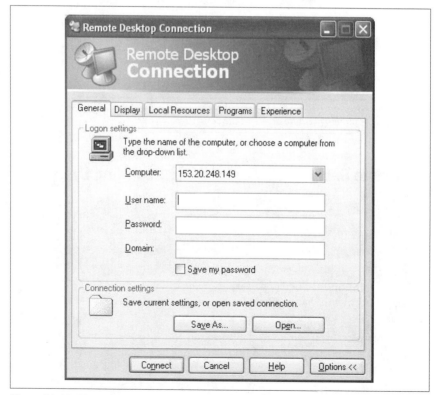

Figure 10-17. Giving access rights to users

Figure 10-18. Using the Remote Desktop to log in to another XP computer

2. Enter the IP address of the remote host and enter the username, password, and domain name (if required). You can click on the various tabs (Display, Local Resources, Programs, and Experience) to customize the options available (such as screen size, audio output, etc.).

3. You can now view the remote display either in a window or full screen.

Figure 10-19. Using RDC (on a Mac) to connect to Windows 2000 Advanced Server

Using Remote Desktop, you can:

- Enable the local filesystem to be made available to the remote host.
- Redirect print jobs from the remote host to the local printer.
- Allow local serial and parallel ports to be accessed by the applications running on the remote host.
- Share the clipboard between the local and remote host.

Index

Numbers

1G cellular networking, 191

1x Radio Transmission Technology (1xRTT), 191

2.5G cellular networking, x, 191, 194

2D RMS, measuring accuracy of GPS receivers, 225

3G cellular networking, x, 191
   GPRS and, 194

8- or 12-channel receivers, 225

802.11 wireless standards, 14–22
   security issues with, 85–90
   terminology of, 22–25

802.11a standard, 15
   pure wireless access points, 94
   vs. 802.11b standard, 16–18
   vs. 802.11g standard, 18

802.11b standard, 15
   configuring PCMCIA cards for, 201–203
   D-Link DI-714P+ wireless router, 103
   frequencies for channels in, 22
   included with AirPanel V150, 239
   interference between Bluetooth and, 128
   pure wireless access points, 94
   vs. 802.11a standard, 16–18

802.11g standard, 15
   D-Link DI-624 Extreme G Wireless Access Point, 96

interference between Bluetooth and, 128

pure wireless access points, 94

vs. 802.11a standard, 18

802.11i standard, xi, 72–74

802.1X standard, xi
   authentication, 74–78, 89
      implementing in Windows XP, 78–84
   as security feature, 89
   support of, by access points, 77
   Virtual Private Networks (VPNs) and, 55

A

absorption of radio waves, 12

Access Point Manager, 81

access points, 91–126
   Bluetooth, 132, 163–168
      configuring, 165–168
      connecting to, 164
      testing the connection, 168
   bridging devices between networks, 100
   communicating using channels, 22
   configuring, 80, 104–117
   default IP addresses, changing, 110
   displaying signal-to-noise ratio for, 48
   dual-band, 18
   generating Wi-Fi maps, 235
   getting associated with, 69
   infrastructure mode and, 22, 24, 240

We'd like to hear your suggestions for improving our indexes. Send email to *index@oreilly.com*.

High Speed Circuit Switched Data
(HSCSD), 201
    Nokia D211 vs. Nokia D311, 202
home network setup, 100–102
host computers
    connecting ViewSonic AirPanel V150
        to, 239–245
    using Remote Desktop
        with, 248–251
    setting up VPNs on, 56
host numbers, 2
HotSpotList web site, 41
hotspots (see wireless hotspots)
HotSync, Bluetooth for, 145–147
HSCSD (High Speed Circuit Switched
        Data), 201
    Nokia D211 vs. Nokia D311, 202
HyperTerminal, creating new
        connection with, 227

I

IBSS (Independent Basic Service Set), 20
ICANN (Internet Corporation for
        Assigned Names and
        Numbers), 5
ICMP (Internet Control Message
        Protocol) requests,
        enabling, 66
IEEE 802.11 standard (see 802.11
        wireless standards)
IEEE TGi workgroup, 72
images
    compressing, 217
    turn off loading, 212
Independent Basic Service Set (IBSS), 20
Infrared Data Association (see IrDA)
infrared technology, x, 174–190
    connecting to
        Internet, 181–184
        Pocket PCs with
            ActiveSync, 179–180
    file transfers, 177–188
    security issues, 188–190
    sharing Internet
        connections, 184–188
infrastructure networks, 22, 24
    configuring WLAN access, 203
    connecting AirPanel to host
        computers, 244

Initialization Vector (IV), 70–72
integrity, 68
    checking for, before encryption, 70
    tunneling and, 55
Intel XScale PX250 processor, 238
Intercom Profile, 136
interference between Bluetooth and
        other devices, 128
interference (radio) and absorption, 12
Internet
    connecting to
        using infrared
            technology, 181–184
        using mobile phones, 148–150
    connection sharing
        troubleshooting, 158
        using Bluetooth, 155–159
        using infrared
            technology, 184–188
        with neighbors, 124
Internet Accelerator by T-Mobile, 218
Internet Authentication Server,
        configuring, 79
Internet Control Message Protocol
        (ICMP) requests, enabling, 66
Internet Corporation for Assigned
        Names and Numbers
        (ICANN), 5
Intersil PRISM-II/Intersil PRISM-2.5
        chipsets, 26
IP addresses, 1–8
    ad-hoc networks and, 120
    assigned by ICANN, 5
    bypassing, 105
    calculating network numbers from, 3
    classes of, 2
    default of access points,
        changing, 110
    DHCP and NAT, 93, 97, 100, 112
    Domain Name System (DNS) and, 7
    filtering, as security measure, 88
    limitations of, 7
    obtaining, 5, 104, 245
        automatically, 111
    opening ports and, 116
    ranges of, 2
    reserved, 3
    resetting, 112
    scarcity of, 102
    static, 111

U

UHF (Ultra High Frequency) band, 10
Ultra High Frequency (UHF) band, 10
UMTS (Universal Mobile Telephone
        Service), 194
unauthorized access points, 103
    detected by NetStumbler, 47, 232
uncontrolled ports, 76
Universal Mobile Telephone Service
        (UMTS), 194
Unix systems, downloading Remote
        Desktop clients for, 249
unsecured wireless servers, connecting
        to, 29
USAPhotoMaps mapping software, 230
USB adapters, 19
    for AirPanel V150, 239–243
    for Bluetooth, 131
    connecting to wireless networks
        with, 37
    for infrared, 175
    troubleshooting, 125
Usenet newsgroups about cellular
        issues, 192
user-to-network VPN, 54

V

Venturi compression software, 218
Verizon Wireless and compressing proxy
        servers, 218
Very Fast Infrared (VFIR), 175
Very High Frequency (VHF) band, 10
Very Low Frequency (VLF) band, 10
VFIR (Very Fast Infrared), 175
VHF (Very High Frequency) band, 10
ViewSonic AirPanel V150, 238–247
    connecting
        peripherals to, 246
        to host computers, 239–245
    docking station for, 239
    expansion slots on, 240
Virtual Private Networks (VPNs), 54–62
VisualGPS software, 230
Vivato indoor wireless switches, 98
VLF (Very Low Frequency) band, 10
voice services
    3G networks and, 194
    GSM networks and, 193
    Sierra Wireless AirCard 750, 200
VPNs (Virtual Private Networks), 54–62

W

WAN IP address, setting, 111
WAP (Wireless Application
        Protocol), 193, 197
Warchalking, 50–52
Wardriving, 49–52
    legality of, 50
    with NetStumbler, safety issues
        for, 233
Warflying, 49
Warwalking, 49
Watcher icon for AirCard 555, 213–216
wavelength of radio waves, 8
waypoints (GPS locations), 224
WayPort hotspots, 43
WCDMA (Wideband CDMA), 191, 194
web-based configuration for access
        points, 105–109
WEP (Wired Equivalent Privacy)
        standard, xi, 22, 70–72
    configuring wireless networks, 107
    dynamic WEP keys, 73
    enabling for wireless networks, 110,
        125
    problems with, 53, 71, 90
    specifying WEP keys, 29
    vs. WPA, 75
WIDCOMM Bluetooth Stack
        driver, 140
Wideband CDMA (WCDMA), 191, 194
Wi-Fi Alliance, 15
    Wi-Fi Zone and, 45
Wi-Fi Protected Access standard (see
        WPA standard)
Wi-Fi technology, x
    generating maps, 235
    putting on notebook
        computers, 14–39
    security issues and, 67–84
    troubleshooting, 125
Wi-Fi Zone, 45
    web site for, 41
WiFinder web site, 41
WildPackets Inc., 87
Windows XP
    Bluetooth technology and, 137–140
    conflicts between D-Link DWL-650+
        and, 35
    implementing 802.1X authentication
        in, 78–84

About the Author

Wei-Meng Lee is an experienced author and developer specializing in .NET. He was awarded the Microsoft Most Valuable Professional (MVP) award (in .NET) in 2003. Besides .NET development, Wei-Meng maintains a keen interest in wireless technologies and has coauthored many books and articles on mobile application development and XML technologies. He is also a contributing author to several trade publications such as *SQL Server Magazine*, *Visual Studio Magazine*, *DevX.com*, and *.NET Magazine*. He currently writes a regular column for the O'Reilly Network (*http://www.oreillynet.com/pub/au/944*).

Contact Wei-Meng at *wei_meng_lee@hotmail.com*.

Colophon

Our look is the result of reader comments, our own experimentation, and feedback from distribution channels. Distinctive covers complement our distinctive approach to technical topics, breathing personality and life into potentially dry subjects.

The item on the cover of *Windows XP Unwired* is a bird cage. When a pet owner invests in a bird cage, he needs to consider certain factors, such as safety and size. A bird pecks at the bars of its cage, so the materials that the cage is made of are important because certain metals are poisonous to birds. Stainless steel is the best type of metal to use; however, if this is not available, there are cages that have a "bird-safe" powder baked on to the metal. This coating protects the bird from any toxins. In terms of the size of a cage, it should be large enough to offer at least double the bird's wing span, from the top to the bottom of the cage as well as from side to side. Ideally, a bird should have even more room than that. In addition, it is sometimes suggested that it is a good idea to provide your pet bird with a large cage for the day and a smaller one for sleep, in order to offer the bird a change of scenery.

Mary Brady was the production editor and the copyeditor for *Windows XP Unwired*. Sada Preisch was the proofreader. Emily Quill, Phil Dangler, and Mary Anne Weeks Mayo provided quality control. Judy Hoer wrote the index.

Edie Freedman designed the cover of this book. The cover image is an original photograph by Edie Freedman. Emma Colby produced the cover layout with QuarkXPress 4.1 using Adobe's Helvetica Neue and ITC Garamond fonts.

David Futato designed the interior layout. This book was converted to FrameMaker 5.5.6 by Andrew Savikas with a format conversion tool created by Erik Ray, Jason McIntosh, Neil Walls, and Mike Sierra that uses Perl and XML technologies. The text font is Linotype Birka; the heading font is Adobe Helvetica Neue Condensed; and the code font is LucasFont's TheSans Mono Condensed. The illustrations that appear in the book were produced by Robert Romano and Jessamyn Read using Macromedia Free-Hand 9 and Adobe Photoshop 6. This colophon was compiled by Mary Brady.